# Guide to the Bonaire Marine Park

# Guide to the Bonaire Marine Park

a guide for snorkelers and divers

by **Tom van 't Hof**

with color photographs by **Dee Scarr**

drawings by **Heleen Cornet**

*This project was made possible with funds from the World Wildlife Fund Netherlands*

# Photo credits

Color photographs are by Dee Scarr and black and white photographs by the autor, except as credited below.

*Fleur van Duyl*
Figs. 51, 66, 106, 147, 199, 208, 212, 220.

*Tom van 't Hof*
Figs. 31, 79, 134, 145, 152, 158, 217.

*Eric Newton*
Figs. 167, 171.

*Herb Segars*
Fig. 90.

*Cover photo*
Sandy Cober and Christie Dovale at Carl's Hill.

*Printed by:*
Tesink-Holland

*Design by:*
Bert Arts gvn



Published by Stinapa, in cooperation with Orphan Publishing Company - Curaçao.

ISBN 90.70824.01.9

Stinapa Documentation Series No. 11.

# Table of contents

# Foreword

Soestdijk Palace, May 1983.

It gives me great pleasure to introduce the reader to the Guide of the Bonaire Marine Park.

Since the moment in 1974 that the World Wildlife Fund was asked to assist in setting up a 'Pilot Plan' for a Bonaire Marine Park, much of the original plan has been implemented. Financial support from WWF-Netherlands, thanks to their campaign 'Give and care for nature' made this possible. With marine-biologists in control of the Park, its ecological centre efficiently housed in the beautifully renovated mansion 'Karpata', with 44 dive-sites carefully selected, each marked by a buoy, with diving activities on the increase to more than 50.000 dives a year, this 'Diving Guide' means another important step towards the completion of the original blueprint of this truly challenging undertaking.

In view of the diving intensity, this fieldguide signifies a most important tool for the Marine Park visitors who can now enjoy fully the beauty of the underwaterworld without causing any damage to the highly vulnerable ecology of the reefs and its inhabitants. It is for that reason that I recommend the use of this Guide to visitors of Bonaire and most emphatically so to all who want to venture into the fascinating world of Bonaire's coastal reefs. With my compliments to those who contributed to the excellent realisation of this Guide, I wish them great success with its publication and the reader a most rewarding experience!

Bernhard

Prince of the Netherlands.

# Preface

Bonaire is enjoying a real boom in diving. You read something about Bonaire frequently in diving magazines and it seems to have become the number-one diving destination of the Caribbean. Bonaire's star is rising rapidly, and deservedly so. Allow me to explain to you why.

Bonaire has beautiful, highly accessible, fringing reefs that never suffered from overexploitation, pollution or poaching. Spearfishing has been prohibited on this island since 1971. Our dive operations are extremely well-organised, and, even though it occasionally rains on Bonaire, it is true that you can dive 365 days a year. With the establishment of the Bonaire Marine Park along the entire coasts of Bonaire and Klein Bonaire a new dimension was added to those favorable circumstances: a kind of guarantee that every possible effort would be made to keep the reefs as beautiful as they are now.

The island Government is more than pleased with the attention that Bonaire enjoys in the divers' world. Some people however, regret that Bonaire is no longer the quiet, almost primitive island of 10 or 20 years ago.
This is rather shortsighted reasoning. Bonaire needs development to become economically more self-supporting. But not at any price. There is no need for Bonaire to copy other islands. It is unique and can remain unique if developed wisely. I believe the concept of the Bonaire Marine Park reflects wise government.
It means that we do not want to develop the potential of the coral reefs with only short-term profits in mind, but that we are looking for lasting returns.

This book serves essentially two purposes. First of all it helps you to select dive sites, to give you the highest returns from your diving excursions and to guide you through the underwater world. Secondly it helps the park because the Guide is also educational: the more you know about the reefs the more you will appreciate them and the more you will understand about the impact of your behavior on the reef. The Guide does not contain any information on diving and hotel facilities on Bonaire. To obtain such information I suggest that you contact one of the following Bonaire Tourist Boards:
- Bonaire: One Breedestraat, Kralendijk; Telephone 8322 or 8649;
- United States: 1466 Broadway, Suite 903, New York, NY 10036; Telephone 212-869-2004.
- Canada: 815-A Queens Street East, Toronto M4M 1H8, Ontario; Telephone 416-465-2958.
- Venezuela: Torre Maracaibo, piso 15-E Avenida Libertador, Caracas; Telephone 723460 or 723583.

I am grateful to all the people who helped in one way or the other to realize this guide. First of all I wish to thank Franklin Winklaar who has been my diving buddy on nearly all dives and who was also Dee's buddy for many of the dives on which she took photographs for this book. He never complained about the long hours underwater even though he was sometimes shivering with cold. Franklin also accounted for a considerable portion of the darkroom work for the Guide. Fleur van Duyl allowed me liberal access to the unpublished data collected in connection with her reef mapping project. Her aerial photographs and draft maps were an excellent aid in the preparation of some of the maps and descriptions. She also critically read the manuscript and suggested several improvements to the text. Rolf Bak of the Caribbean Marine Biological Institute in Curaçao and my colleague Eric Newton of the Bonaire Marine Park also commented on the manuscript. Dee Scarr became more and more involved in the preparation of the manuscript. She not only made numerous corrections to the text but also contributed to the sections on fish life, wrote about individual fish characters and is the author of the sections on night diving and fish feeding. Aubrey Tiel of the Caribbean Marine Biological Institute deserves special credit for photographing the illustrations and for the final printing of all black-and-white material. Mrs. Phyllis Koeyers diligently typed the different versions of the manuscript.

The preparation of this Guide was an important part of the marine park project. I have worked on the guide with immense pleasure and sincerely hope that using this Guide will give you the same kind of satisfaction.

The author.

**The author**
*Tom van 't Hof* (38) started diving when he was 16. He wanted to study oceanography, but this was impossible in Holland. He obtained a Master's degree in biology from the University of Amsterdam and served several years as coordinator of oceanographic research projects in the Caribbean and the North Atlantic. While based in Curaçao he did research on the ecology of soft corals. In 1979 he was asked by the Netherlands Antilles National Parks Foundation to set up a marine park in Bonaire.
He is presently based in Curaçao as project leader of the Curaçao Underwater Park.

**The photographer**
*Dee Scarr* holds MA and BA degrees in English and public speaking, and taught highschool in Florida for 6 years. Abandoning that life for the lure of the sea in 1977, she has worked as a dive guide in the Bahamas and Bonaire.
An increasing interest in marine animal behavior prompted Scarr to initiate *Touch the sea,* a program of personalized dive guiding, on Bonaire in 1982. She has had articles and photographs published in several dive magazines and is currently writing a book on the *Touch the sea* concept.

# Chapter 1

## Conservation and the Bonaire Marine Park

Marine Parks in general and coral reef parks in particular are relatively new in the history of park development. Even though some of the older marine parks date back to 1940, the majority was established in the seventies. This is not so surprising when you realize that we have only begun to explore, understand and enjoy the shallow marine environment since SCUBA became available, some 30 years ago. On the other hand the post-World War II demographic explosion with a concurrent need for increased exploration and exploitation of mineral and living resources, has led to misuse of the marine environment. The rapid post-war industrialization and the favorable economic development of the industrialized world, allowing for higher wages and shorter workhours, has resulted in demands for more opportunities to spend all the free time. Development has had an undeniable impact on the environment: industries have ejected harmful substances into the seas, living resources have been overexploited or even depleted, the coastal zone has been rapidly developed for industrial settlement and for recreational purposes - often at great costs to the marine environment - to satisfy the needs of millions that want to spend their money and free time.

Fortunately, our children are no longer brought up in an era in which conservation is considered a luxury and development *always* has priority over conservation issues. Today we are beginning to understand that development and conservation are not conflicting issues, that they are supplementary, at least if we want to guarantee lasting returns from development and exploitation. In other words that we have to manage the environment and living resources if we don't want to see ecosystems destroyed and stocks depleted.

The International Union for Conservation of Nature and Natural Resources (IUCN) and the World Wildlife Fund (WWF) are two international organizations that work together in promoting conservation worldwide. IUCN establishes guidelines and priorities for conservation action, whereas WWF acts as a fundraising organization and funds conservation projects selected on the basis of the criteria set by IUCN. The objectives of conservation were recently defined by IUCN and other international organizations in a document called the 'World Conservation Strategy' as follows:

a to maintain essential ecological processes and life support systems on which human survival and development depend;
b to preserve genetic diversity (the range of genetic material found in the world's organisms), on which depend the functioning of many of the above processes and life support systems;
c to ensure sustainable utilization of species and ecosystems.

In recent years IUCN and WWF have directed considerable attention to marine conservation. Among the projects that were approved and funded by IUCN and WWF is the Bonaire Marine Park.
In 1979 the Netherlands Antilles National Parks Foundation (better known by its Dutch acronym STINAPA) received a grant from WWF-Netherlands for a project to develop and establish a marine park in Bonaire. The main objective of reef conservation in Bonaire is to maintain the coral reef ecosystem, as well as the seagrass and mangrove systems of the lagoon Lac with their high biological productivity and esthetical values in order to ensure continuing returns from fishing and recreation at sustainable levels. In other words one needs to be able to control - to a certain extent - the use of the reef ecosystem and to ban those activities that are known to be harmful to the marine environment. This can be achieved by legislation and enforcement. It means certain restrictions as to the use of the reef system, but these can be kept to a minimum. One has to design a management program in which all the tasks that aim at achieving the objective of reef conservation have their place. Along these lines the contours of a marine park are shaped.

*Fig. 1*
*Oil pollution: a continuous threat to the coastal and marine environment.*

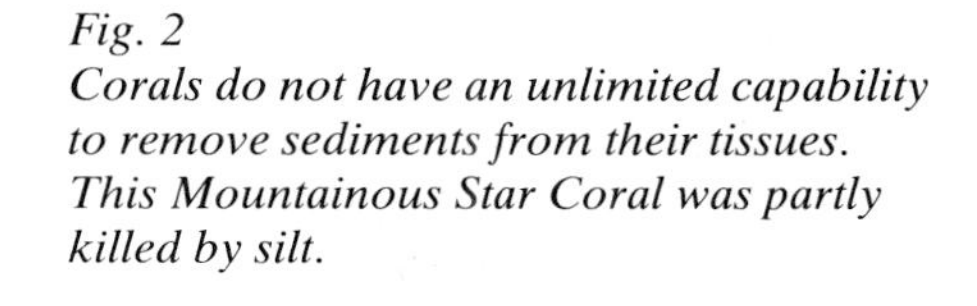

*Fig. 2*
*Corals do not have an unlimited capability to remove sediments from their tissues. This Mountainous Star Coral was partly killed by silt.*

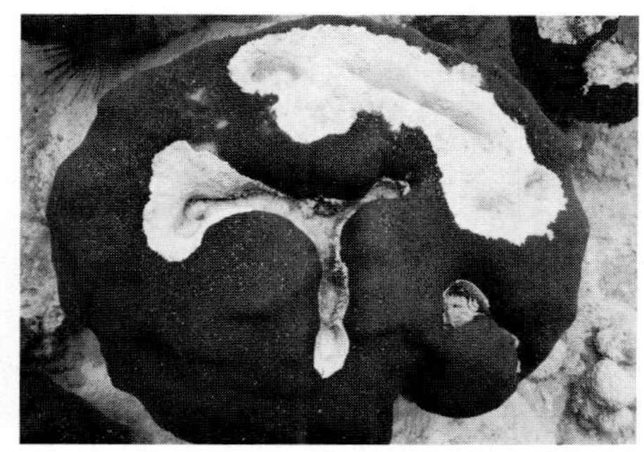

*Fig. 3*
*Anchors wreck coral; in the Bonaire Marine Park anchoring in the coral is not allowed.*

*Fig. 4*
*Reef conservation in Bonaire is timely; the reefs are virtually untouched and coral growth is lush.*

*Fig. 5*
*Reef fish are in abundance in Bonaire (snappers at Angel City).*

*Fig. 6*
*Public moorings prevent anchor damage and provide safe anchorage for the boats of the dive operators, fishing boats and pleasure boats.*

The entire coast of Bonaire and Klein Bonaire is lined with coral reefs. They appear like a tiny fringe around a mountain of which the top is just emerging above the surface, surrounded by deep oceanic water. Because they are only such a narrow fringe, they are extremely vulnerable: harmful activities on land are likely to affect the whole reef system. Even though not all reefs around Bonaire are equally threatened by developments or activities that can be deleterious to them, *all* reefs of Bonaire were declared a marine park. This was done for two reasons mainly: there appeared to be relatively few conflicting uses of the reef system, and, control is facilitated. For example, if coral collecting is prohibited in the marine park and the park only included the reefs of Klein Bonaire, a diver caught outside his hotel or home unloading some fresh trunks of black coral could allege to have collected it outside the park boundaries. By applying the same regulations to all reefs this is not possible. For the purpose of legislation and control the Bonaire Marine Park is defined as the *seabottom and the overlying waters from the highwater tidemark down to the 60 m (200 ft) depth contour.*

We should make it clear that an important characteristic of marine conservation in Bonaire is that it is *timely.*
It happens more often than not, that action is taken when it is too late. There are numerous examples of reefs that are virtually depleted of fish by spearfishing or the use of other detrimental fishing methods such as dynamite; where corals, including black coral, and shells are collected in unlimited amounts to be sold as souvenirs, or even corals are extracted from the reef to be used as building material, and where reefs have been smothered with silt as a result of dredging and filling. In Bonaire we were on time. You will find its reefs virtually untouched, with coral growth lush and fish populations abundant.
For this reason Bonaire has become popular as a diving destination and for this very reason we must make every effort to ensure that its value as such is not adversely affected by development.

What exactly makes the Bonaire Marine Park different from 'the coral reefs, surrounding the islands of Bonaire and Klein Bonaire'? Basically the fact that activities are controlled by legislation and that there is a management program for the marine environment. However, to be able to understand that this is a slight understatement we must tell you a little bit about the different aspects of the management program. It includes:
1 research and monitoring: such as research on the impact of coastal development, on the impact of resource exploitation in the park and monitoring of visitor-related impacts;
2 advice to the Island Government, based on the results of research and monitoring, on marine resource management, on the need for temporary closing of certain areas if recreational pressure becomes too high or on the need for revising the existing legislation or preparing additional legislation;
3 law enforcement; policing the park;
4 the provision of services and facilities to users, such as park interpretation through brochures, lectures, slide presentations, films, self-guided underwater trails (will be set up in the future), *this* guide, a visitor information center (at Karpata) and permanent moorings to provide safe, environmentally harmless anchoring at the dive sites.

To a large extent the 'services' aim at creating a better understanding and knowledge of the coral reef. We believe that awareness and appreciation of the coral reef as a fragile ecosystem will automatically lead to a more environmentally conscious attitude among the visitors. In this connection we would like to encourage you to visit the exhibition and aquarium at the 'Karpata Ecological Center'. This center in the restored plantation house of Karpata serves as the administrative headquarters of STINAPA and the Bonaire

Marine Park, as visitor information center for the marine park and as a facility for ecological research as it relates to park management.

We owe you an explanation about two areas within the marine park that are closed for diving and snorkeling and are called reserves. We have selected and set aside two areas strictly for research purposes. To be able to monitor visitor-related impact we need areas where no recreational activities take place and that can be compared with others receiving a high recreational pressure.
They were selected on the basis of conformity with 'stressed' areas and not because of special features. The areas are located in between Karpata and Gotomeer and in between Playa Frans and Boca Slagbaai (see map). They are buoyed and marked as closed reserves. All we ask is your cooperation.

All this information about the background of marine conservation and the Bonaire Marine Park doesn't make sense unless we also tell you about the park rules. You may be interested in this background information and remember some of it while you are diving, or you may not, but you still must remember the park rules.

**Bonaire Marine Park: Park rules** (The park stretches all along Bonaire and Klein Bonaire down to 60 m-200 ft-depth)

1 Respect the marine environment and engage in no activities that may damage it (don't sit or step on corals - they are living animals! -, control your movements and your buoyancy).
2 The marine life is completely protected; there is no collecting (except for fishing with handlines or fishing rods and hand-catching of non egg-bearing Spiny Lobster above 25 cm - 10 inches - total length).
3 Spearguns and of course, spearfishing, are not allowed.
4 Anchors wreck coral and anchoring is not allowed in the coral (except for emergency anchoring and anchoring by boats of less than 3.6 m - 12 ft - using a stone as anchor); between shore and the drop-off in the Town harbor area is an extensive sand-bottomed bay where anchoring is permitted.
5 Artifacts cemented into the reef substratum may not be taken.
6 Fast boats are not allowed in Lac; their propellers whirl up silt and damage the seagrass beds.
7 Do not dive or snorkel in the marine reserves (the buoyed areas in between Karpata and Gotomeer and in between Playa Frans and Boca Slagbaai).
8 The mooring system is a public service; handle the moorings with care and remember that they are designed in such a way that, in order to be safely anchored, you must pay out extra line when tying to a mooring.

Let the motto be, no matter whether you are an experienced SCUBA diver or snorkeling on a reef for the first time in your life: 'Watch, learn, understand and above all ENJOY'.

# Chapter 2

# Introduction to the Bonaire reefs and their ecology

**A bit of geological history**
The island of Bonaire originated in a series of submarine volcanic eruptions that took place more than 70 million years ago. The island emerged from the sea and became exposed to erosion, waves pounded its shores, and reefs began to develop. Remnants of the oldest reefs are the slightly tilted hills that can be seen in the north-west of the island (for example the Wasao, just west of Gotomeer). The exposed and eroded limestone terraces testify to more 'recent' reef development and were formed during periods of sealevel changes combined with continuous slow uplifting of the island. In these terraces you can see many corals that you will also encounter on the living reef (clearly visible for example in the large rocks that broke off the cliff in the northern corner of Boca Slagbaai).

**The coast**
There are basically two coastal types on Bonaire:
a A steep cliff, found in the greater part of the northern half of the island, and,
b A low coast with coral rubble beaches or beachrock and calcareous sand, in the southern half of the island.

When you are driving along the scenic road towards Gotomeer you will notice a notch, a few meters above the level of the road, which was formed during a former sealevel at the air-sea interface. The notches are formed primarily by grazing and boring organisms that live in this zone and remove limestone in a process called 'bioerosion'. These processes are also at work today and you can see notches in the seaward edge of the cliff when you are diving one of the sites along the scenic road (fig. 7).
Another interesting phenomenon can be seen along the north coast where the cliff is exposed to big waves generated by the trade-winds. In the middle of the notch a bench, also called sawah-bench, has developed (fig. 8). Here calcareous algae and worm shells that prefer the turbulent water of the surf, cap the limestone with a hard impenetrable layer that delays erosion in relation to other parts of the cliff. Examples of these benches can be seen all along the north coast.

**Reefs along the leeward side of Bonaire and along Klein Bonaire**

*Reef profile*

Regardless of the type of coast you will always find a narrow, gently sloping, shallow submarine terrace that extends seaward to a drop-off at about 10 m (33 ft)

*Fig. 7*
*Cross-section through the cliff along the leeward coast. Notches are formed in the air-sea interface by bioerosion; notch (a) corresponds with a past sea-level, notch (b) is formed at the present sea-level.*

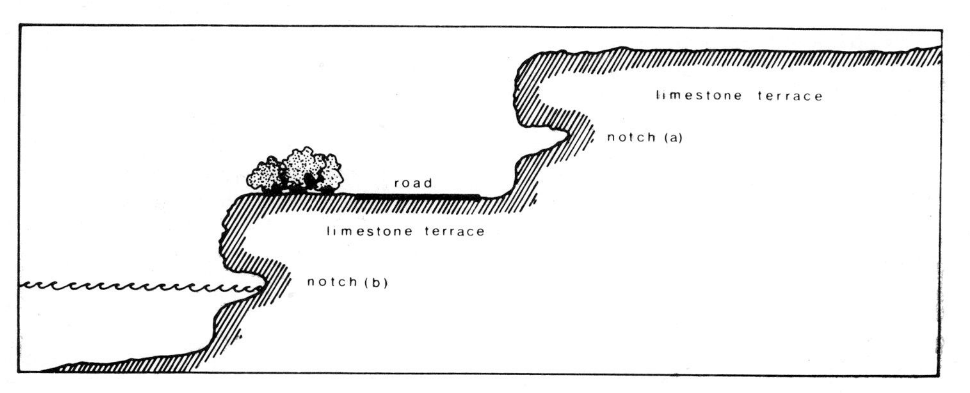

*Fig. 8*
*Cross-section through the cliff along the windward coast. The bench in the middle of the notch represents an area of retarded erosion.*
*A and B correspond with different levels of exposure to wave action: with highest exposure (B) the cliff above the bench lies entirely in the spray zone and is eroded.*

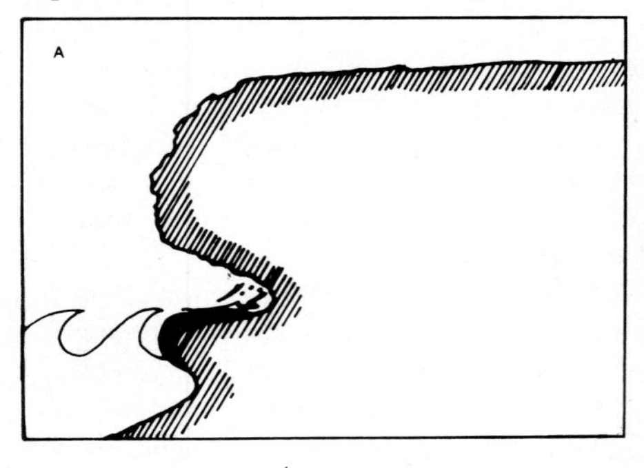


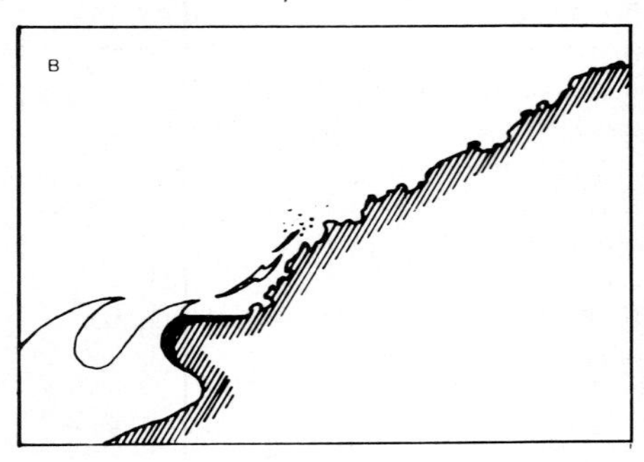


*Fig. 9*
*Buttress formation at La Dania's. Sediment is transported downslope through the valley in between the two buttresses.*

and is followed by a slope, varying in angle from 30° to vertical, down to a depth of 30 to 60 m (100 to 200 ft). At that depth there is usually a sand terrace and a second drop-off at 50 to 80 m (170 to 270 ft). Below a depth of 80 m (270 ft) hardly any reef-building corals occur. Don't consider this information as an encouragement to explore the deepest part of the reef. We simply want to give you a complete picture of the reef.

The reef profile does not consistently follow the same pattern along the entire coast:

1 The width of the terrace varies between 20 and 160 m (70 and 530 ft); it is relatively wide along the southern part of Bonaire's west coast (dive sites 2 through 8), along the west coast of Klein Bonaire (dive sites 17 through 20) and the east coast of Klein Bonaire (dive sites 12 and 27), and relatively narrow along the north coast of Klein Bonaire (dive sites 21 through 26) and the south-west coast of Bonaire (dive sites 34, 36, 37, 38 and 39);

2 The drop-off depth is fairly constant with one exception: along the east coast of Klein Bonaire the drop-off begins at 1-2 m (3-7 ft); (dive sites 12 and 27).

3 Vertical reef slopes are found in a few places. The most extensive wall is at La Dania's (38), others are Small Wall (32), Cliff (31), Carl's Hill (21) and Rappel (37).

4 A second reef has developed in places where the reef slope ends relatively shallow, that is at a depth of 30 m (100 ft) or less. The second reef is separated from the slope by a sand channel (dive sites 4 through 8).

5 Although not influencing the overall reef profile, some structures strike as different from the general pattern: on various dive sites you will find *buttresses,* coral promontories growing outward of the reef and running from the drop-off down along the reef slope, with alternating sand *valleys* (fig. 102). The buttresses are quite steep in places and have a very high cover of living coral. Buttress formation is

*Fig. 10*
*Reef profile and general pattern of coral zonation along the leeward coast.*

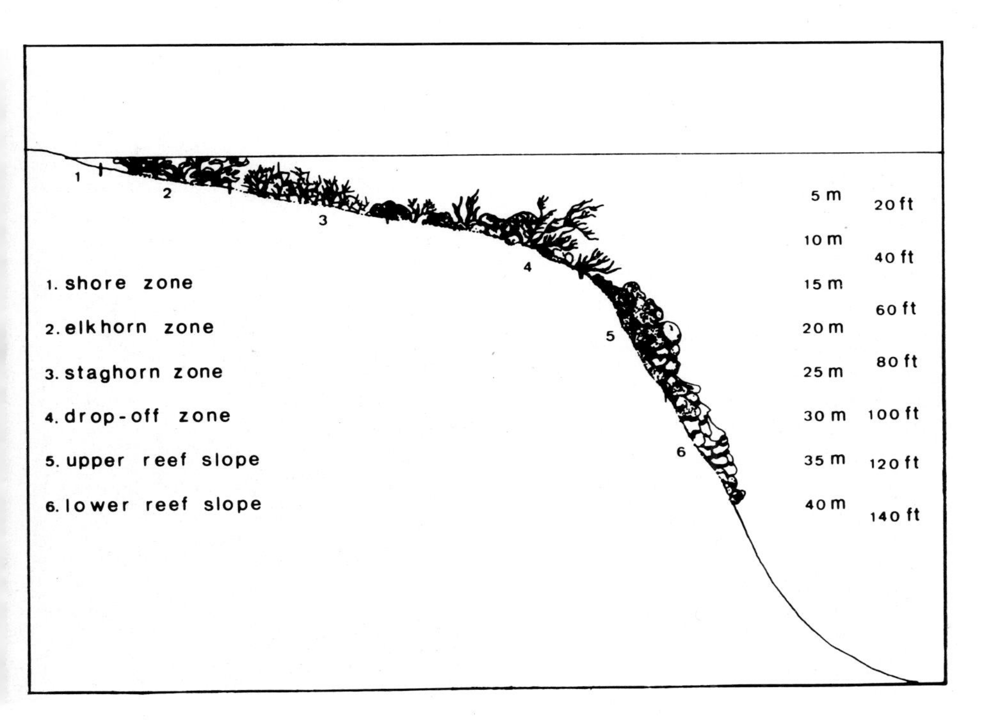


well-known from the reefs of Jamaica and the Cayman Islands where buttresses have grown seawards and sidewards so much that neighboring buttresses have joined and formed tunnels. Sand is transported down the reef slopes through the valleys and consequently they make a very unstable substratum, not suitable for coral settlement.
Toppling and sliding down of large coral heads at the drop-off as a result of bioerosion may be partly responsible for the formation of these valleys. There are indications that the spacing of buttresses follows a certain pattern and is related to water movement. The best examples of buttress formation are found at Forest (16), Ebo's Reef (27), La Dania's (38), Karpata (39) and between Slagbaai and Wayaka (41). Structures, resembling the buttresses and valleys, but occurring in shallow water with strong wave action are called *spurs and grooves* (fig. 222). They are spaced closely together and oriented perpendicular to the wave front. Spurs and grooves are found at Playa Bengé (43) and Boca Bartól-south (44). They are believed to be formed by a combination of seaward and upward growth of corals and erosive forces.

## *Coral Zonation*

Most coral species have a fairly wide vertical distribution, but obtain their greatest abundance within a specific depth range. Thus we can use different coral species or groups of species to distinguish different zones on the reef. Slightly generalizing we can identify the following pattern of zonation (fig. 10).
1 *Shore zone,* between 0 and 1 m (3 ft), characterized by encrusting Knobby Brain Coral, adapted to the strong water movement of the surf.
2 *Elkhorn zone,* from 1 to 4 m (3 to 13 ft), dominated by the Elkhorn Coral. Elkhorn Coral hardly occurs beyond this zone. Fire corals and crustose coralline algae are also abundant in this zone. Along the southern

*Fig. 11*
*Knobby Brain Coral, characteristic of the shore zone.*

part of the west coast (dive sites 2 through 8) the Elkhorn zone is inconspicuous as Elkhorn Coral occurs infrequently or is even absent. In other places however, Elkhorn Coral is so dense that it forms a massive barrier. Such a barrier consists mainly of dead Elkhorn Coral, covered with and cemented together by crustose coralline algae, with living coral only at the top and the edges of the barrier. Examples are Nukove (40) and Petries Pillar (33).

3 *Staghorn zone,* from 4 to 7 m (13 to 23 ft), dominated by Staghorn Coral. Interspersed with the Staghorn Coral are often fire corals, Yellow Pencil Coral, small head corals (brain corals and Mountainous Star Coral) and, to the seaward edge of this zone, gorgonians (gorgonians, also called soft corals, are related to stony corals but lack the hard limestone skeleton). The Staghorn zone is often unclear or even absent in places where the shallow terrace is narrow. It is then called the 'barren zone'.

4 *Drop-off zone,* from 7 to 12 m (23 to 40 ft), characterized by gorgonians just above the drop-off and Mountainous Star Coral at the drop-off. Large patches of Yellow Pencil Coral also occur in this zone. The upper part of the drop-off zone may be somewhat barren. In the lower part of this zone Flower Coral becomes more abundant.

5 *Upper reef slope,* 12 to 25 m (40 to 83 ft), dominated by Mountainous Star Coral and Leaf Coral. Giant Brain Coral and Smooth Starlet Coral also cover a significant portion of the available space. In the upper part of this zone Flower Coral and patches of Yellow Pencil Coral are often found.

Typical of this zone are the high buildings of Mountainous Star Coral, sometimes towering like Chinese pagodas above the reef face and creating considerable relief. They occur mostly in a knobby columnar growth form above the drop-off and in a smooth, spherical or shingle-like form below the drop-off. Their color can be

*Fig. 12*
*Elkhorn Coral at Playa Bengé.*

*Fig. 14*
*Staghorn Coral.*

*Fig. 13*
*Barrier of Elkhorn Coral just below the surface (Petries Pillar).*

*Fig. 15*
*Drop-off zone at Rappel. Mountainous Star Coral, mostly in knobby columnar growth form, with gorgonians; Giant Brain Coral in the center of the picture.*

*Fig. 16*
*Patches of Yellow Pencil Coral occur in the drop-off zone.*

pale tan or bright green. They are often excavated as a result of bioerosion and eroded at the base, bound to fall over sooner or later because of their own weight and weakened attachment. Gorgonians are more or less restricted to the upper part of the reef slope (along with the shallow terrace and drop-off of course). However, they are remarkably abundant on the reef as a whole in the southern part of the island (dive sites 1 through 8) and along the south-western tip of Klein Bonaire (dive sites Forest, 16 and South-west Corner, 17). They seem to thrive best in areas with strong water movement. For example the dark-reddish fan-shaped Deepwater Gorgonian is only found in places where strong currents (strong according to Bonairean standards) occur, such as Red Slave (2), Forest (16), Playa Bengé (43) and Boca Bartól (44).

6 *Lower reef slope,* from 25 m (83 ft) down, often characterized by a 'roof-shingle' community composed of Sheet and Scroll Corals and some Mountainous Star

*Fig. 17*
*Upper reef slope at Jerry's Jam/Ebo's Special dominated by pagodas of Mountainous Star Coral.*

*Fig. 18*
*Roof shingle community of the lower reef slope. Sheet Coral in the foreground left. Mountainous Star Coral shingles in the center and Black Wire Corals in the background.*

Coral in a flattened growth form. With increasing depth only a few coral species, notably Cavernous Star Coral, Blushing Star Coral, Sheet and Scroll Corals remain abundant, and crustose coralline algae occupy most of the available space. Cavernous Star Coral and Sheet Corals are abundant on vertical walls, even in relatively shallow water. This is not so strange as the reduced light intensity on vertical slopes and overhangs imitates the deep reef environment.
Two species of black coral are common on the lower reef slope: Dichotomous Black Coral and Pinnate Black Coral, the former being the species most wanted for jewelry making*. The optimum depth for Dichotomous Black Coral is more shallow (25-

* Any black coral collecting on Bonaire and Klein Bonaire is subject to license by the Government. Sofar only the Handicraft Center has obtained a permit to collect certain amounts of black coral from an area that has a low recreational potential. Penalties for poaching coral on Bonaire include a maximum fine of NAf. 5,000.– or 2 months imprisonment.

*Fig. 19*
*Spotted Cleaning Shrimp associated with Pink-tipped Anemone.*

*Fig. 20*
*'Mob' of surgeonfish and Yellow Goatfish foraging in the staghorn zone.*

*Fig. 21*
*Schooling of Smallmouth Grunts near the Staghorn Coral at Calabas Reef.*

30 m/83-100 ft), than for its pinnate relative (40-45 m/133-150 ft), but the former is low in numbers in the southern half of the island and virtually absent along the windward coast. Black corals are abundant around Klein Bonaire, notably at Forest (16) and Ebo's Reef (27) and in the northwestern part of Bonaire.
The coral zonation on the reef slope is sometimes not clear or absent. For example in places where the reef slope is short (that is ends between 24 and 30 m-80 and 100 ft) the roof shingle community, typical of the lower slope, will not be present.

We can hear those who have diligently studied these pages, exclaiming after their first dive: 'It's not like the book says at all!'. Fortunately not. Or the reefs wouldn't offer you such a variety of structures and coral communities as they in fact do. We have given you a general pattern along with some variations to the theme to help you recognize some common trends in the way the reef is built.

*Zonation of other invertebrates and fishes*

As to other reef invertebrates and fishes it is even more difficult to give you a general picture of what you might expect in different parts of the reef. However, certain animals show a preference for certain habitats.
If the *shallow terrace* has an elkhorn barrier you will see, besides numerous Long-spined Sea Urchins, Redlip Blennies sitting on the pink algal crusts. The Jewelfish (juvenile of the Yellowtail Damselfish) with its iridescent blue spots, hides in between the plates of the fire corals and Leaf Corals.
In the Staghorn zone but also on sand rubble bottoms the Pink-tipped Anemone is abundant. Shrimps like Pederson's Cleaning Shrimp, Spotted Cleaning Shrimp and Little Brown Spotted Shrimp are often associated with this anemone, while juvenile fishes seek protection near the tentacles. Extremely common in this zone is also the Common Lettuce Slug. It feeds on algae that grow on dead staghorn branches. Commonly appearing in the staghorn zone are the Coney, Rock Hind, Butterflyfish and Damselfish. Especially the Yellow or Three-spot Damselfish defends its small territory with fervor and will not hesitate to attack animals many times its size (such as divers).
Browsing parrotfish and surgeonfish are typical of the shallow terrace. They scrape algae off the coral limestone with their specialized teeth. You can often see surgeonfish foraging in schools, moving rapidly from one place to another; parrotfish, goatfish, sometimes a Spanish Hogfish or a Trumpetfish move along with them. Wrasses are present everywhere on the shallow terrace and in the drop-off zone. Furthermore you will see the Rock Beauty, French Angelfish and Queen Angelfish.
Wherever the terrace is sandy or a combination of sand and rubble you are likely to see the Peacock Flounder that blends in perfectly with the sandy bottom but shows blue-purple rings on its body when disturbed, and the Yellowhead Jawfish (dive site no. 25, Sampler). The Yellowhead Jawfish hovers slightly above the entrance of its burrow and backs into it, tail first, when you come closer. If panicked it dives into the burrow head first. At night it will close the entrance with a pebble.
Also highly typical of rubble areas are the Bicolor Damselfish and the Pygmy Angelfish which is fairly common on Bonaire. You will see lots of both between Hotel Bonaire and the Marina (dive site no. 29). Over a sandy bottom you can see goatfish, probing the sand for food with their barbels, and the Yellowfin Mojarra that sucks in the sand with its snout. Lizardfish and Scorpionfish are likely to be found in areas with dead coral, because they offer more opportunities for camouflage. The Scorpionfish is so well-camouflaged that it often takes a trained eye to spot it. Schooling behavior of the Smallmouth Grunt, the French Grunt and the Yellow Goatfish can be observed near patches of Staghorn Coral on an otherwise sandy bottom (Salt City, 4, Calabas, 10, Sampler, 25).

*Fig. 22*
*Sergeant Major guarding his nest. The large dark patch indicated by the arrow represents the eggs.*

*Fig. 23*
*Black-and-white Sea Lily or crinoid, a filter-feeding Echinoderm.*

Among the gorgonians towards the *drop-off,* especially when a lot of Slimy and Dry Sea Plumes are present, you are likely to see the Basket Starfish. During the day it appears like a bird's nest entangled in the branches of the gorgonian. At night it expands its arms, that are divided many times to form an efficient filtering system (fig. 123).
The Long-spined Sea Urchin remains abundant throughout the drop-off zone, its numbers declining along the reef slope. Typical for the blue water in the drop-off zone are schools of chromis, hovering above the reef and feeding on plankton. The Sergeant Major is also abundant especially if many excavated coral heads are present (dive sites: La Machaca, 30, South Bay, 14 and Calabas Reef, 10). The Sergeant Major uses these excavations to lay its eggs. The nests are visible as purple hues on the coral limestone. The behavior of the male guarding the eggs against predators is so frantic that it will attract your attention and lead you to the nest. Of

*Fig. 24*
*Marbled Grouper, not common on Bonaire.*

the wrasses the Creole Wrasse becomes abundant in the drop-off zone and along the reef slope. Yellowtail Snappers are certainly present but not restricted to this zone: they will follow divers everywhere they go hoping for a handout. In areas with fairly strong water movement, such as Forest (16), Playa Bengé (43), and Boca Bartól (44) the Black Durgon, a triggerfish, is common in the drop-off zone. On the bottom you will commonly find the Graysby, a small grouper, and this is also the place to start looking for Moray Eels.

Along the *reef slope* you can find a variety of Sponges.
Purple Tube Sponges are present almost everywhere, some with over 40 individual tubes (Southwest Corner, 17, Carl's Hill, 21 and Punt Vierkant, 8). Striking are the large orange sponges at Ebo's Reef (27) and the great density of Do-not-touch-me Sponges between Hotel Bonaire and the Marina (Front Porch, 29).
Two species of crinoids (also called sea lilies or feather stars) are common: the Black-and-white Sea Lily, attached to protruding corals and sponges, fully exposed during the day, and the Orange Sea Lily that lives partly hidden in crevices. With the fine pinnules on their arms they filter water for plankton and other food particles.
Look also for Banded Coral Shrimp, displaying their antennae like white whiskers from under a plate of Sheet Coral.
Among the fishes that you are likely to encounter along the reef slope are different species of groupers: Tiger Grouper and Yellowmouth Grouper, common everywhere, big Yellowfin Grouper, not common but widely distributed and an occasional Nassau or Marbled Grouper.
Furthermore jacks, both the Bar Jack and the very inquisitive Horse-eye Jack, that is often seen in schools, snappers (Yellowtail Snapper, Schoolmaster, Mahogany Snapper and Grey Snapper) and the Scrawled and Whitespotted Filefish. Black Margates are occasionally seen at many dive sites but are extremely abundant at Angel City

Fig. 25
*Grey Snapper (foreground) and Black Margates at Angel City.*

Fig. 26
*The shallow terrace along the north coast is covered with the brown alga* Sargassum.

(6). All these fishes are in the blue water or just above the reef itself; within the coral you will see Spotted Moray Eels commonly and an occasional Green Moray Eel.
Few fishes are strictly confined to one particular zone. They just seem to be more common in one than in an other.

**The windward reefs**
Because of the trade winds the windward side of Bonaire is normally too rough for diving. For this reason we have included only one dive at the southern end of the windward coast, Lighthouse (1), in this guide. But you may happen to be here during a calm period (short, infrequent periods which occur between August and December) and then it is certainly worthwhile to make one or two dives on this side.
The shallow terrace is rather wide and invariably covered with extensive fields of the brown alga *Sargassum platycarpum*. Sargassum may extend as deep as 30 m (100 ft). Where the coast is formed by a cliff, the cliff can continue vertically below the surface down to 10 or 15 m (33-50 ft). The drop-off is not very distinct in most places: often the beginning of the reef slope is only marked by a slight increase in angle. With a few exceptions the reef slope is gentle. Coral cover is nowhere high. Coral growth is continuous along the southern part of the windward coast but becomes patchy in the northern part. Besides the Sargassum many gorgonians, especially the Common Sea Fan, occur on the shallow terrace along with encrusting corals such as the Knobby Brain Coral and the Smooth Starlet Coral. There is no staghorn zone, but Elkhorn Coral occurs dispersed at depths between 5 and 15 m (17and 50 ft). Coral growth is most prolific between 10 and 25 m (30 and 83 ft) where you will see huge Giant Brain Corals, and large flattened Mountainous Star Corals along with gorgonians. Algae dominate the deep reef. Big groupers are far more common than on the leeward side and you

*Fig. 27*
*Elkhorn Coral in* Sargassum *bed along the north coast.*

will see Southern Stingrays, Queen Triggerfish, big Grey Snappers, Rainbow Parrotfish, Spiny Lobster and many other creatures that are unusual on the leeward coast.

**The dynamics of reef building**
Although reefs are commonly considered highly developed, mature and stable ecosystems, the processes involved in shaping the reef are very dynamic. Coral reefs are confined to shallow tropical seas with little fluctuation in temperature and salinity. You will not find coral reefs on most of the western sides of the continents where cold water is brought to the surface by upwelling, nor near the outflow of large river systems. Coral reefs have been destroyed or severely damaged by the hot effluents of power plants, by the hot and saline effluents of desalination plants and by the construction of airports, harbors, marinas and beaches where dredging and filling released huge amounts of silt and resulted in an increased turbidity of the water. You will not find coral reefs in the deep sea, although coral species are represented in the deep ocean basins. Apparently light is a very important factor in reef building. This is accounted for by a symbiotic relationship of the reef-building corals with unicellular algae, called zooxanthellae. The relationship is mutually beneficial.
The zooxanthellae, like all plants, carry on a process called photosynthesis (in photosynthesis water and carbon dioxide, in the presence of light combine to form carbohydrates and oxygen).
Thus the zooxanthellae provide the coral polyps with carbohydrates. Also by using the coral's waste carbon dioxide, the zooxanthellae lower the acidity inside the polyp, facilitating the formation of the coral's skeleton (which is composed of calcium carbonate - limestone, hence the name 'stony' corals) by the polyps. The polyp delivers carbon dioxide, a waste product of its metabolism and ammonia, an other waste product that contains the

*Fig. 28*
*Divers should not sit on coral heads: corals are living animals!*

essential nitrogen, to the algae and gets rid of its waste products in an easy manner. Only corals with zooxanthellae are capable of depositing limestone in sufficient quantities to build reefs.

So corals, together with lime-secreting algae, are the primary reef-builders. At a cover of 100% they can produce about 100 tons of limestone per ha per year (40 tons per acre per year).

Their degree of success as reef constructors depends on such factors as reproduction, the possibilities for settlement of their larvae, predation and competition. The larvae released by a coral must find a suitable place to settle within a few weeks or they will die, insofar as they have not already fallen prey to carnivores. The struggle for life goes on.

The young coral is virtually defenseless against predators and the competition with other reef invertebrates for space is ruthless. If it manages to survive these difficult stages of its early life the coral will grow by budding off new polyps and by producing limestone for its skeleton, a slow process in most coral species. Coral polyps feed by stretching their tentacles at night and grasping planktonic organisms that come too near. After years they reach sexual maturity, but even for adult corals many imminent dangers remain.

Snails like the Short Coral-shell and the Chocolate-lined Top-shell eat live coral. You will see Fire Worms ingesting a branch of Staghorn Coral; when they are finished a white (dead) tip is left. Small white scars on corals can be caused by predation by the Long-spined Sea Urchin or by herbivorous fish incidentally munching away living coral tissue. Unfortunately divers are often partially responsible for coral damage because they hold to corals or step or sit on them. Small scars will heal fairly easily but bigger scars may be colonized by algae or sponges before they heal. Any dead surface will make the coral susceptible to settlement by boring sponges and algae. The boring sponges are especially effective: they create a system of tunnels and galleries

*Fig. 29*
*Red Boring Sponge.*

*Fig. 30*
*Urchins graze on the algae that grow on dead coral limestone and can excavate large coral heads.*

in the coral's skeleton and remove some 5-10 tons of limestone per ha per year (2-4 tons per acre per year) of the limestone laid down by the corals (once dead coral limestone is covered by crustose coralline algae it becomes impenetrable to boring sponges). Wherever scars remain unhealed long enough fleshy algae settle on the dead surface. Sea urchins and herbivorous fishes such as parrotfish browse on these algae at the same time scraping off substantial amounts of coral limestone. Especially the Longspined Sea Urchin can be seen to excavate large coral structures. Herbivorous fish and urchins together remove about 25 tons of limestone per ha per year (10 tons per acre per year).
In spite of this bioerosion there is a net accumulation of limestone resulting in a slow upward growth of the reef as a whole. This growth is estimated at 1-4 mm (1/25-1/6 inch) per year, depending on the coral cover.
Another form of reef degradation is brought about by a phenomenon that we call *reef slide.* In some places you will notice gaps in the reef at the drop-off. The reef slope below such a gap is usually sandy with rubble and broken dead corals. This is the result of such a reef slide: not just a large coral head tumbled down but the whole reef face broke off at the drop-off and slid down. Good examples of reef slides are found at Jerry's Jam/ Ebo's Special (22) and Knife (24).
The slide east of Knife is about 30 m (100 ft) wide.

In addition to sexual reproduction for some coral species asexual reproduction seems to be an important means of propagation. For example, broken fragments of Elkhorn Coral will survive, attach themselves and continue to grow provided that they do not suffer too much from scouring over the bottom.
This is an important aspect of the life strategy of a coral species that, because of its shallow occurrence and growth form, is periodically destroyed by storms. Add to this that the Elkhorn Coral grows faster

*Fig. 31*
*The white band disease seriously affected the Staghorn Coral in 1980 and 1981.*

*Fig. 32*
*Field of healthy Staghorn Coral before the white band disease.*

*Fig. 33*
*Juvenile fish sheltering in between the tentacles of a Pink-tipped Anemone.*

than almost any other coral and you have a picture of how corals are equipped by nature to cope with the problems they are likely to encounter.

In their competition for food, light and space the corals possess a unique mechanism: they can attack and kill each other. Not randomly, but in accordance with a hierarchy whereby one coral species is dominant over the other. When two corals belonging to different species grow close together and touch each other, the contact area will show a white rim: the dominant coral has killed its neighbour's polyps in this area and will eventually overgrow the other. The actual killing is done by expelling the polyp's mesenterial filaments, that contain digestive enzymes, over the neighbor's tissues. Sometimes the attacked coral reacts to the aggression with the formation of long so-called sweeper tentacles in the contact area (well-known for example of Cavernous Star Coral).

Besides competition, predation and aggression, diseases can also affect corals. For example the Staghorn Coral - and to a lesser extent the Elkhorn Coral - have been seriously affected by a disease, the so-called white-band disease, that first manifested itself in the summer of 1980. The disease caused the death of at least 75% of all Staghorn Coral on the Bonaire reefs. However, as of the spring of 1982 we observed some recovery of this coral species and we are fairly confident that, by the time this guide is revised, the Staghorn Coral will look healthy and pretty again on most places.

**Relationships among reef inhabitants**

To reach the present complexity and degree of variation the coral reefs have gone through various stages of development.

Gradually the number of species on the reef increased. Most steps undertaken in the evolutionary process were aimed at conserving energy, making the system more efficient. One of these steps was to try interrelationships between different species, which in some cases would become true interdependencies.

The best known relationship is probably parasitism, in which only one of the partners benefits at the cost of the other. Common examples of parasitic relationships on the reef are the Yellow and Red Boring Sponge infesting coral skeletons, especially at the base of a colony (the Yellow Boring Sponge is recognized by its small, low, bright yellow pipes, the Red Boring Sponge is encrusting, has symbiotic colonial anemones, and occasional large segmented oscules). Or the isopods attached to the skin just below the eye of the Creole Fish (on Bonaire only the Creole Fish is affected by this large isopod).
There are also relationships in which both partners benefit (for example cleaning symbiosis) or relationships beneficial to one of the partners and neither to the advantage nor to the disadvantage of the other (for example juvenile fish seeking shelter in between the tentacles of an anemone or the spines of a sea urchin).

We already spoke of one, very important, relationship on the reef, that between the coral polyps and algae, a clearly mutually beneficial one. Other widely-spread symbiotic relationships are cleaning symbiosis, the association of shrimps with anemones, symbiotic colonial anemones living on sponges and the 'menagerie' of small invertebrates and fish living inside sponges.

Cleaning symbiosis is a ritual in which certain shrimps and small fishes relieve bigger fishes of parasites. The ritual is introduced by the cleaner calling attention to its presence by an unusual behavior, and / or by a special behavior or change in coloration of the fish that wants to be cleaned to attract the attention of potential cleaners. Common cleaners are gobies, juvenile Spanish Hogfish, juvenile Bluehead Wrasses, Pederson's Cleaning Shrimp, Spotted Cleaning Shrimp and the Banded Coral Shrimp. Cleaning usually takes place at fixed points along the reef, the so-called cleaning stations. Large

*Fig. 34*
*The cleaning of a Tiger Grouper by a goby.*

*Fig. 35*
*Tiger Grouper in very pale coloration at a cleaning station. The arrow indicates one of the cleaners, A Banded Coral Shrimp.*

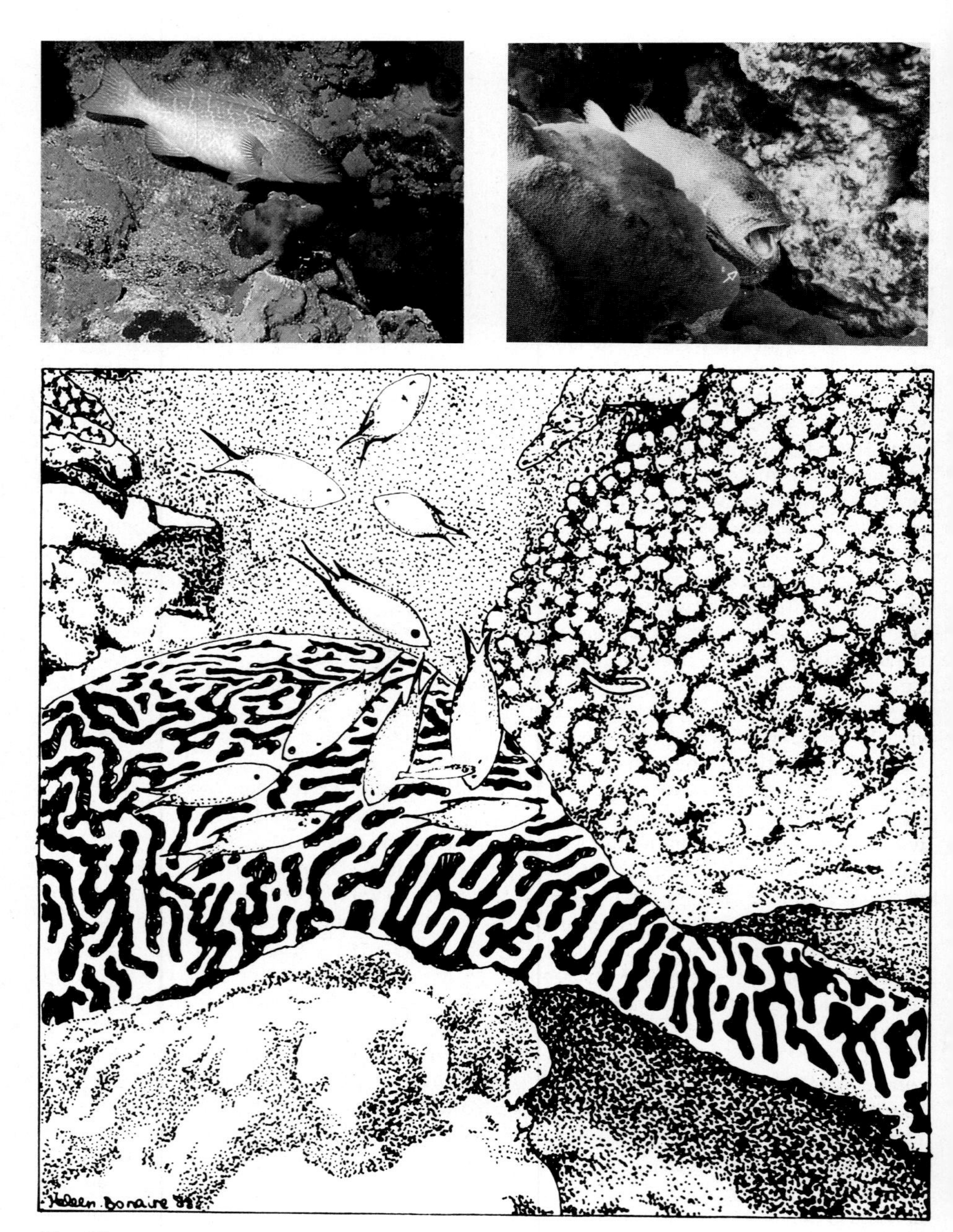

*Fig. 36*
*The cleaning ritual often involves a special behavior. These Brown Chromis indicate their desire to be relieved of parasites by a headdown position.*

conspicuous boulders of Mountainous Star Coral often serve as cleaning stations. Moray Eels are mostly cleaned by shrimp; groupers by shrimp, gobies and sometimes a Spanish Hogfish all at the same time. You will see chromis and Creole Wrasses cleaned by juvenile Spanish Hogfish and Bluehead Wrasses, and jacks specifically by Spanish Hogfish. With a little patience you can even have your own fingers cleaned by the shrimp or Neon Gobies. The only way to observe cleaning is to spot a cleaning station from a distance. If you get to within 2 or 3 m (6-10 ft) of a cleaning station you will have disturbed the ritual. Once you have spotted a cleaning station move in closer very carefully and if you disturb the cleaning, draw back a little bit and wait quietly for the fish to resume their positions.

The shrimps that are associated with anemones obviously derive protection from this symbiosis. Their immunity to the nematocysts (stinging cells) of the anemone is not an inherited feature but must be acquired by gradually 'getting in touch' with the anemone.

Some sponges are so densely covered with anemones that you wonder what they actually are. They are indeed sponges, but living in symbiosis with symbiotic colonial anemones. Quite a few species of sponges have them and they benefit from the relationship because the anemone produces substances that are toxic to certain fishes and may keep them from preying on the sponge. Sponges are also hosts to myriads of other animals that apparently benefit from the water current that the sponge creates by its pumping action. One peculiar example is a small goby that lives in the Do-not-touch-me Sponge and swims seemingly tireless against the outgoing current in the large openings. It must be a very beneficial relationship to justify all the energy spent on it.

These few examples are just an illustration of the complexity of the system. The more we get to know about the reef, the more we understand that very few things happen randomly. Most events seem to be part of some grand scheme. Although this complexity may be an advantage in terms of economics, it is certainly a disadvantage in terms of vulnerability of the system. Changes and disturbances imposed on the system from the outside, may in fact, because of all these relationships and interdependencies, affect the entire system.

# Chapter 3

## Dive site descriptions

*Fig. 37*
*Vertical reef slopes are found at Carl's Hill, Cliff, Small Wall, Rappel and La Dania's Leap.*

**Introduction**

Most divers stay only one week on Bonaire (but come back frequently). You cannot possibly dive all 44 dive sites in one week, although we know people who have crammed about half that number in one week. To help you select your dives, we have grouped the dive sites into 5 categories according to the characteristics of the reef; a 6th category includes the sites that don't fit any of the other categories. You will notice that there is some overlap: for example we consider Nearest Point a 'typical' reef, but it also has buttresses, so it is listed under the category 'buttresses' too. With the help of the map and/or the alphabetical index of dive sites, you can trace the page number of any dive site description, as long as you know its name or reference number.

**Categories of dive sites**

| *Category* | *Characteristics* | *Dive site* |
|---|---|---|
| 1 Typical | Shallow terrace with Elkhorn Coral, Staghorn Coral or a barren zone, gorgonians in the drop-off zone, Mountainous Star Coral dominant in upper reef slope and Sheet and Scroll Corals in the lower slope (provided the slope extends deep enough). | 9 Windsock Steep<br>10 Calabas<br>13 Nearest Point (also 2)<br>14 South Bay (also 2)<br>17 South-west Corner<br>18 Twixt<br>19 Valerie's Hill<br>20 Mi Dushi (also 2)<br>21 Carl's Hill (also 4)<br>23 Leonora's Reef (also 2)<br>24 Knife<br>25 Sampler<br>26 No Name (also 2)<br>30 La Machaca<br>33 Petries Pillar<br>34 Oil Slick Leap<br>35 1000 Steps<br>36 Ol'Blue<br>40 Nukove<br>42 Playa Funchi. |
| 2 Buttresses | Usually a steep reef slope with buttresses developing from the drop-off down, alternated with valleys through which sediments are transported down the slope. | 12 Just-a-nice-dive<br>13 Nearest Point (also 1)<br>14 South Bay (also 1)<br>15 Hands-Off (also 6)<br>16 Forest<br>20 Mi Dushi (also 1)<br>23 Leonora's Reef (also 1)<br>26 No Name (also 1)<br>27 Ebo's Reef<br>38 La Dania's (also 4)<br>39 Karpata<br>41 Slagbaai to Wayaka |

| Category | Characteristics | Dive site |
|---|---|---|
| 3 Short reef slope and/or double reef. | Reef slope with a mild angle, 'deep' sand terrace begins relatively shallow. Lower slope community absent, gorgonians abundant throughout the reef. On most places a second reef, separated from the reef slope by a sand channel, has developed (we refer to dive sites 4 trough 8 as the 'Alice in Wonderland' double reef complex). | 3 Pink Beach<br>4 Salt City<br>5 Alice in Wonderland<br>6 Angel City<br>7 The Lake<br>8 Pt. Vierkant |
| 4 Wall dives | Vertical reef slopes | 21 Carl's Hill (also 1)<br>31 Cliff<br>32 Small Wall<br>37 Rappel<br>38 La Dania's (also 2) |
| 5 'Specials' | Unusual or sensational fish life, invertebrate life or reef structures. | 1 Lighthouse<br>2 Red Slave<br>11 Town Pier<br>22 Jerry's Jam<br>41 Slagbaai South<br>43 Playa Bengé<br>44 Boca Bartól |
| 6 Other | Does not fit any of the other categories. For characteristics refer to individual dive site descriptions. | 15 Hands Off (also 2)<br>28 Something Special<br>29 Front Porch |

Each description includes a list that contains general information on the dive site. In order to save space the meaning of the numbers 1 through 10 is not printed with the description. Instead we give you an explanation below, and for handy reference you can use the bookmark that also explains the numbers.

1 *Boat dive or shore dive* (or both).
Sites without a mooring, where anchoring in the sand is not possible, must be considered shore dives. Mooring buoys carry the names and numbers of the dive sites. Yellow stones along the road, also provided with names and numbers, help you to find the location of dive sites from the shore.

2 *Type of mooring and mooring depth*

3 *Type of entry* (applies to shore dives only).

4 *Approximate distance from shore to the drop-off* (shore dives only)

5 *Classification according to diving skills*
The majority of the dive sites can be dived by anybody who has an open water diving certificate. A few sites are classified as 'experienced' or 'highly experienced'.

6 *Depth of the drop-off*

7 *The degree of cover by corals* is expressed

using a relative index (low, fairly low, moderate, fairly high, high, very high). Only stony corals are considered, dead or alive, in estimating the cover.

8 *Recommended dive direction.* If one side relative to the point of entry is preferred over the other, we have indicated so. As a general rule you swim upcurrent; you can follow the recommended dive direction insofar as it matches with the upcurrent direction or if there is no current (currents are mild in Bonaire; for exceptions we refer you to the dive site descriptions). Indications of direction like 'east' or 'west' are accompanied by 'left' of 'right'; that is, facing the sea.
This heading also refers you to the carry-along waterproof reef maps, if available for that particular dive site.

9 *Recommended maximum diving depth* (RMDD). On most dive sites there is no need to go deep. As you will see the RMDD does not exceed 24 or 27 m (80 or 90 ft) on most dives, about the depth where the roof shingle community begins. Of course there is more to see below that depth, but in most cases nothing that justifies the hazards of deep diving. Occasionally we indicate an exceptional depth as RMDD, for instance in the Boca Bartól description. We realize that we have recommended a decompression dive, but we think it is worth it; that is, if you feel completely prepared for a deep dive. On guided dives you simply stick to the rules imposed on you by the dive operator.

10 *Value of dive site for snorkeling.* This will aid snorkelers in deciding which reef trip to sign up for, as well as help those going out on their own to select good snorkeling sites.

As a rule each description has the following sub-headings in this order: drop-off zone, upper reef slope, lower reef slope, shallow terrace, fish life. This is done because you will begin your boat dives close to the drop-off, go down along the slope first, then come back up and save the shallow terrace for the last part of your dive. In the case of typical shore dives however, we describe the shallow terrace first. We only use this classification insofar as it makes sense. If there is nothing special to tell about the drop-off zone, we don't include that sub-heading; if the reef slope is short, the lower slope lacking and a double reef present, we arrange the text accordingly; if a certain aspect of the fish fauna is totally linked to a certain habitat, we combine it with the description of that habitat rather than dealing with it under a separate heading. You will notice that we have capitalized common names of species mentioned. This is done to avoid ambiguity about the species meant. Any capitalized name refers to one single species. Invertebrate and plant names used in the text can be found in the list of common names on page 144 together with their scientific name and possible synonyms. Names like parrotfish, groupers, fire coral, black coral and sea fan are collective names that include a number of different species and are not capitalized.

In several instances we use swimming time as an indication of distance. We realize that swimming speed will differ from person to person, however we feel this is the best choice to give some indication of distance. Our swimming times are based on relaxed swimming by a diver who stops regularly to take notes or photographs.

By including sections on individual fish characters in the reef descriptions we have taken a risk: that next month or next year that particular fish will no longer be there. We used to see 'Dushi', a tame Marbled Grouper, between South-west Corner and Valerie's Hill, and one morning Dushi was no longer there.
After a 4 month absence, we now think he may be back - but at Forest! Despite these problems, we wanted to introduce you to our fish personalities. Even if the fish have moved on, the introduction will give you

*Fig. 38*
*'Dushi', a tame Marbled Grouper, used to be seen between South-West Corner and Valerie's Hill.*

an idea of the animal-human friendships possible on Bonaire.
In general, describing a given fish with a given reef has its problems. One day we will all see the Green Moray Eel, the next day it just isn't there. You dive once more the place where you saw that school of Horse-eye Jacks: not a single one.
Our descriptions are based on experience of several hundreds of dives, and yet you will not see all the things that we describe. On the other hand we are sure you will see lots of other things that we don't describe. It all depends on how you are 'tuned'. One person may be tuned to fish behavior, the other to macro-invertebrates, someone else again to the 'landscape', the structure of the reef in general. All three will see different things when diving the same reef. Our own perceptions of the reef have gradually evolved over a period of many years. Ask three cold-water divers to make a description of, let's say Angel City and you will end up with three completely different descriptions. Yet it is the same reef.
We have kept you long enough now, let's go diving!

*Fig. 39*
*Green Moray Eel.*

# Dive site:
# **Lighthouse** (Willemstoren)

*Fig. 40*
*Shallow-water community characteristic of the east coast: very lush gorgonian fauna with abundant Common Sea Fans.*

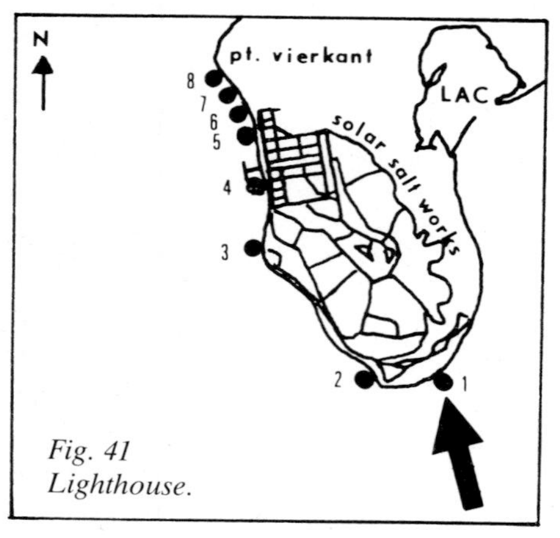


*Fig. 41*
*Lighthouse.*

1 *Shore dive*
2 *none*
3 *fairly difficult; easy in calm season*
4 *90 m (300 ft)*
5 *experienced (because of difficult entry)*
6 *10-12 m (33-40 ft)*
7 *fairly high in the drop-off zone, low on the reef slope*
8 *south-west (right, facing the sea)*
9 *15-18 m (50-60 ft)*
10 *limited snorkeling value unless sea is calm.*

**Description**

We recommend this site to the experienced diver only because the entry is normally rough. A good swimming ability is required to swim through the surf. During calm weather, however, this site can also safely be dived by the less experienced diver. The trick is to restrict an upright position to the absolute minimum: start swimming as soon as you have sufficient depth, diving under the breaking waves, and, at the end of your dive, keep swimming as long as you can, then take off your fins and quickly walk towards the shore before a big wave knocks you over. Although this dive site is called 'Lighthouse' there is no need to enter exactly at the lighthouse. You could enter at almost any point in between the old seawater intake (visible as a straight, narrow, abandoned canal 700 m - 2300 ft - east of the slave huts) and the lighthouse.

Down to a depth of 2 m (7 ft) the *shallow terrace* consists of flattened rock with some algae and Knobby Brain Coral. Gradually gorgonians, the Common Sea Fan in particular, and stony corals such as the Smooth and Knobby Brain Coral and Smooth Starlet Coral become more abundant. Note that all Common Sea Fans are oriented perpendicular to the direction of the waves and have a strong, horizontally extended attachment to the bottom. From about 3 m (10 ft) down the terrace is densely covered with gorgonians, stony corals and the brown alga *Sargassum*. From about 4 m (13 ft) you will see some Elkhorn Coral and a few colonies of Staghorn Coral. You will notice that the Longspined Sea Urchin is absent in this area.

Coral and gorgonian growth is most lush and diverse in the *drop-off zone,* from about 7 m (23 ft) to 15 m (50 ft), and includes abundant sea plumes, false plexaura, Common Sea Fans, Leaf Coral, Giant Brain Coral, Mountainous Star Coral, Smooth Starlet Coral and Yellow Pencil Coral.

Along the *reef slope* below 15 m (50 ft)

Fig. 42
Tub Sponge.

cover by living coral is low and algae, small gorgonians and sponges dominate the scene.
Deepwater Gorgonians and Tub Sponges are particularly common along the reef slope. A deep sand terrace with numerous gorgonians and sponges begins at 39 m (130 ft).

*Fish life.* Grazing parrotfish and surgeonfish are abundant above the drop-off. Squirrelfish are hiding in the holes and crevices in the shallow terrace. Midnight Parrotfish are not exceptional here. Fish are especially plentiful down to about 15 m (50 ft): here you will see numerous Schoolmasters, Mahogany Snappers, Bluestriped Grunts, Coneys, Yellow Goatfish, an occasional Queen Triggerfish or a Barracuda or a Spotted Moray. Black Durgons are common in the drop-off zone. Along the reef slope you see abundant Blue Chromis, several small groupers (Coney, Graysby), large Tiger Groupers, some Nassau Groupers and an occasional big snapper. It is quite clear that the fishes are not used to any handfeeding in this area.

*Fig. 43*
*The Queen Triggerfish is not uncommon along the windward coast.*

# Dive site:
# **Red Slave** (Oranje Pan, Pietiké, Peliké)

*Fig. 44*
*Grey Snapper.*

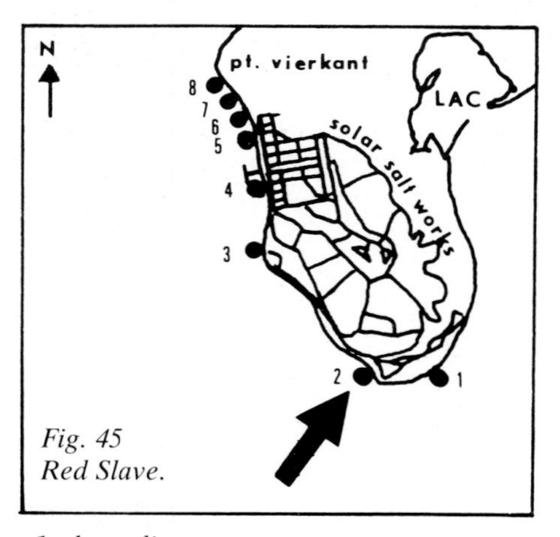


*Fig. 45*
*Red Slave.*

1 *shore dive*
2 *none*
3 *reasonable*
4 *90 m (300 ft)*
5 *experienced*
6 *9 m (30 ft); down to 12 m (40 ft) to the south, up to 6 m (20 ft) to the north*
7 *low to moderate*
8 *south (left, facing the sea)*
9 *27 m (90 ft)*
10 *limited snorkeling value.*

**Description**
A dive site for those who want something different. You get there by driving south from town, past the solar salt works until you reach the second set of slave huts. Enter right behind the slave huts opposite the small parking lot. Entry will normally not be difficult, but we do not recommend this site for unexperienced divers because strong currents (strong by Bonairean standards) may occur. Direction of current is variable due to the formation of eddies at the tip of the island but tends to be south.
There are old anchors, ballast stones and other archaeological artifacts in this area. Remember that it is not allowed to take any artifacts that are cemented to the reef face. Quite a few cannon and anchors have been salvaged in 1968 and 1970. These originated from HMS BARHAM that ran aground here in 1829.
There are supposedly more cannon, still buried in the sand.

You swim out over a *shallow terrace* of flattened hard rock, covered with a thin layer of sand and an algal turf, and next over patches of rounded coral fragments. From 3 m (10 ft) down all the way to the drop-off the bottom is a completely barren sand flat, where you will only see some Yellowfin Mojarras foraging in the sand. Deeply cut sand valleys run down the reef slope from the drop-off. Diving here has an element of mystery, of adventure. The deep water looks greenish and large snappers or groupers appear unexpectedly as dark shades.

The *reef slopes* south and north (of the center of the slave huts) are quite different. Towards the south (left, facing the sea) the sand channels discontinue, gorgonians (the not too common stout gorgonian Nodding Plexaurella and the Deepwater Gorgonian - the latter typical for strong currents - occur here) are abundant along the entire reef slope and a variety of sponges is found. Black corals and crinoids are also present, but the black coral does not seem to be very healthy, maybe as a

*Fig. 46*
*Inquisitive Horse-eye Jacks.*

result of silt. Coral cover is not high, nor is the percentage of living coral. Further south the coral cover increases, as well as the number of gorgonians.

Although the abundance of gorgonians is certainly the most conspicuous aspect of the reef itself, the most spectacular part is the large number of big *fish*. On one dive we recorded several large Tiger Groupers, a 1.20 m (4 ft) Yellowfin Grouper, several Nassau Groupers (not common on Bonaire), a school of more than 100 Horse-eye Jacks, 1.20 m (4 ft) Grey Snappers, Black Margates, a school of 18 Midnight Parrotfish, a Southern Stingray and a Hawksbill Turtle, to name only the most spectacular things. Yellowtail Snappers are also abundant but do not crowd in front of your camera here.

To the north (right, facing the sea) you will find an increasing number of deeply cut sand valleys. Although gorgonians and sponges are initially abundant and coral cover is fairly high on the buttresses that alternate with the valleys, the reef slope becomes progressively less attractive as you head north. Also, don't expect to see the same number of big fish here.

# Dive site:
# **Pink Beach** (White Pan, Cabajé)

*Fig. 47*
*Iridescent blue sponge* (Callyspongia plicifera)

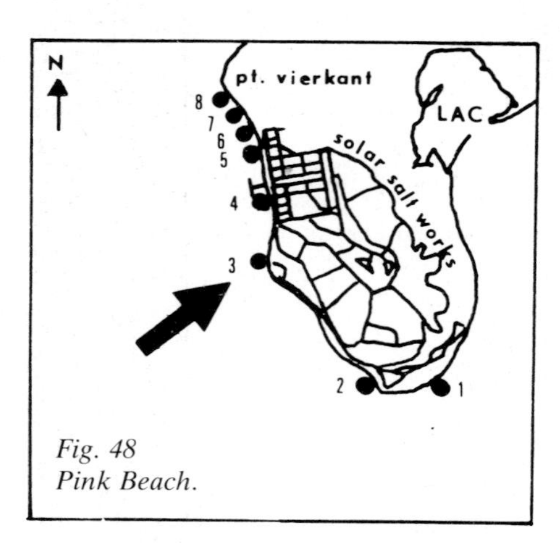


*Fig. 48*
*Pink Beach.*

1 *Boat or shore dive*
2 *double barrel mooring and scrap iron chained together/ 4.5 m (15 ft)*
3 *very easy*
4 *120 m (400 ft)*
5 *all levels*
6 *10 m (33 ft)*
7 *moderate*
8 *either way (current usually going south)*
9 *27 m (90 ft)*
10 *fair snorkeling value*

**Description**
To reach Pink Beach by car you drive south from town, past the condensers of the solar salt works until you reach an abandoned salt barn and a large white house with slave huts next to it. The beach, not visible from the road, stretches north of the salt barn. You can park near the salt barn or anywhere along the road. The mooring site is taken as the starting-point for this description, and is situated off the center of the beach. The beach was named for the color of the sand: the pink color is especially striking when you look at the beach from the water in the late afternoon.

The *shallow terrace* is wide, gently sloping and all sand down to a depth of 4 m (13 ft). Staghorn Coral stretches all the way from 4 m (13 ft) to about 9 m (30 ft). Seaward of the mooring the Staghorn Coral is interspersed with numerous gorgonians.

The *reef slope* is quite attractive with lush gorgonian growth and colorful sponges. Black corals are few. A sand terrace with Garden Eels begins at 27 m (90 ft). The sand flat is also a good place to look for the Sand Tilefish. It hovers closely over the bottom and dives into its burrow head-first when disturbed.

When you swim to the south (left, facing the sea) you will notice that the shallow terrace is nearly all sand, with only patches of Staghorn Coral. You can even find some Garden Eels in the sand above the drop-off there. When you go north (right, facing the sea) return just above the drop-off to enjoy a dense gorgonian forest. You will pass the remnants of three towers of Mountainous Star Coral and a living tower of the same species. They are nesting sites for the Sergeant Major and the large living tower is a cleaning station occupied by several juvenile Spanish Hogfish. In addition it houses Royal Grammas, Black Margates, an Octopus and a Rock Hind.

*Fish life* is abundant. A huge Barracuda (over 1.50 m - 5 ft) is sometimes present

*Fig. 49*
*Juvenile Spanish Hogfish cleaning the body of a Bar Jack.*

and Southern Stingrays are often seen here.
There are schools of Goatfish, Mahogany Snappers, Grey Snappers, Yellowmouth- and Tiger Groupers, an occasional Nassau Grouper, Porgies, Horse-eye Jacks, Spotted Moray Eels and many more.

*Fig. 50*
*School of Yellow Goatfish and Mahogany Snappers among lush soft coral.*

# Dive site:
# **Salt City** (The Invisibles, Saliña Abou)

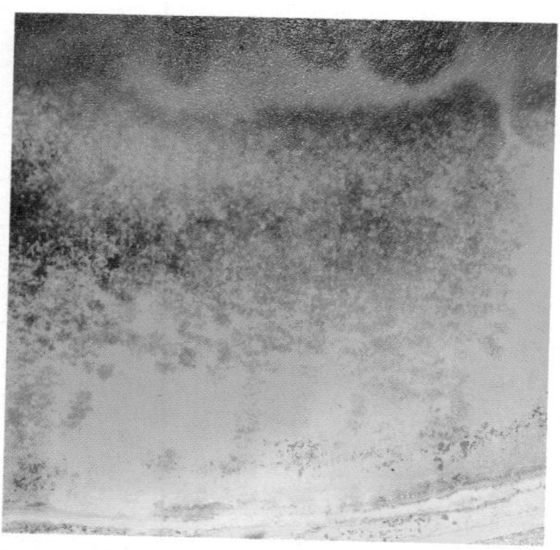

*Fig. 51*
*Aerial view of the southern part of Salt City. Note the sand river in the right part of the photograph.*

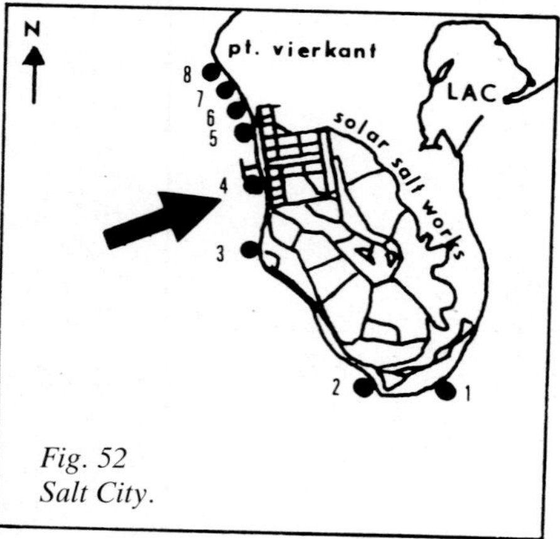


*Fig. 52*
*Salt City.*

1 *Boat dive or shore dive*
2 *double barrel mooring/ 9 m (30 ft)*
3 *easy*
4 *140 m (460 ft)*
5 *all levels*
6 *10 m (33 ft)*
7 *moderate (reef slope) to high (coral 'islands')*
8 *from the mooring: south (left, facing the sea) from shore: see reef map and description*
9 *24 m (80 ft)*
10 *limited snorkeling value*

**Description**
This site is situated at the southern end of the Alice in Wonderland double reef complex. The second reef is discontinuous here and consists of a series of isolated coral outcrops varying in length from a few meters to 150 m (500 ft).
We advise you to clip the waterresistant reef map to a slate and carry it along on your dive. You get here by car by driving south from town just past the loading pier of the Antilles International Salt Company. The dive is described as if it were made from the shore entry point, 450 m (1500 ft) south (left, facing the sea) of the large buoy just south of the salt loading pier.

The *shallow terrace* is fairly wide. Right off-shore the bottom consists of hard rock with scattered Elkhorn Coral, Mustard Hill Coral, fire corals and some gorgonians. Somewhat deeper you will find Staghorn Coral alternated with patches of sand. Grunts often school at the edge of the Staghorn Coral. From 6 m (20 ft) down towards the drop-off there is first a mixed gorgonian-Staghorn Coral community and then a mixed gorgonian-Mountainous Star Coral community.
The wide sand patch that is clearly visible from your shore entry point tapers to the drop-off and flows like a sand river down the reef slope into the sand terrace at 21-24 m (70-80 ft).
The best way to dive from the shore entry is to follow the left 'bank' of the sand river down the reef slope until you spot the 18 m (60 ft) 'island', and then cross the sand to the island.
Diving from the Salt City buoy you will see the second reef as you get down to the sand flat at 21 m (70 ft) at the seaward edge of the reef slope.

The *reef slope* does not have a high coral cover, but lush gorgonian growth. The slope is short: nowhere in between the salt loading pier and the shore entry point is the sand plateau deeper than 30 m (100 ft). All over the sandy plateau you will find Garden Eels and Sand Tilefish. From the shore entry and the small coral island at

*Fig. 53*
*Reef map of the Salt City double reef. Distances along the straight line not to be used for scale.*

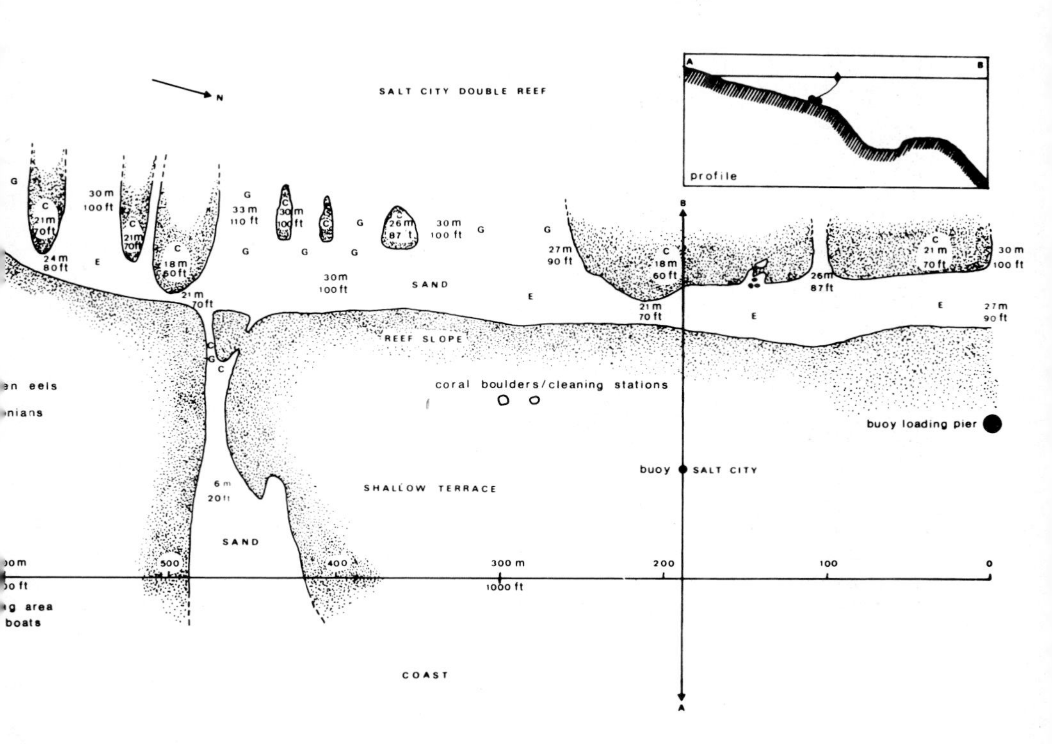


18 m (60 ft) you swim north (right, facing the sea) over a deep (33 m - 110 ft) sand channel to three smaller coral outcrops and subsequently over a sand flat with scattered gorgonians to the biggest coral island that rises 3 to 9 m (10 to 30 ft) above the sand (see fig. 53). All coral islands are extremely pretty, have lush coral growth and abundant sponges. Whichever direction you dive, return shallow. At 6 m (20 ft) are two big boulders of Mountainous Star Coral that are cleaning stations.

*Fish life* on and over the coral islands is sensational. Common encounters are schools of scad and curious Horse-eye Jacks. We have seen a school of Palometa on a number of occasions over the small island at 18 m (60 ft). There are many Tiger Groupers, Yellowmouth Groupers and Graysbys, Nassau Groupers and big Yellowfin Groupers. Schoolmaster and Mahogany Snapper are common. Grey Snapper, Porgy and Black Margate may also be seen. Even the rare (for Bonaire) Grey Angelfish has been observed occasionally in this area.

You wil not regret more than one dive here, there is plenty to explore.

*Fig. 54*
*Palometa.*

# Dive site:
# **Alice in Wonderland**

*Fig. 55*
*This Seahorse was found in the same gorgonian at Alice in Wonderland for six months.*

**Description**
This site is part of the double reef complex that extends from Pt. Vierkant to about halfway to the condensers south of the salt loading pier. The two reefs are separated by a sand channel approximately 35 m (120 ft) wide.

The *reef slope* is lush with different types of corals and rather abundant gorgonians in the upper slope. Coral cover is fairly low. The reef slopes down gently to a depth of 27 m (90 ft), where the sand channel begins. When you cross the sand channel, look for a Garden Eel colony, with eels' heads out of their burrows, swaying curiously into the current.
Also in the channel you might see a Queen Conch or two foraging in the sand, or the Southern Stingray buried in the sand. Small schools of Goatfish and an occasional lone trunkfish also investigate the sand for food.

Soon the contours of the *second reef* will become visible out of the blue. Where you

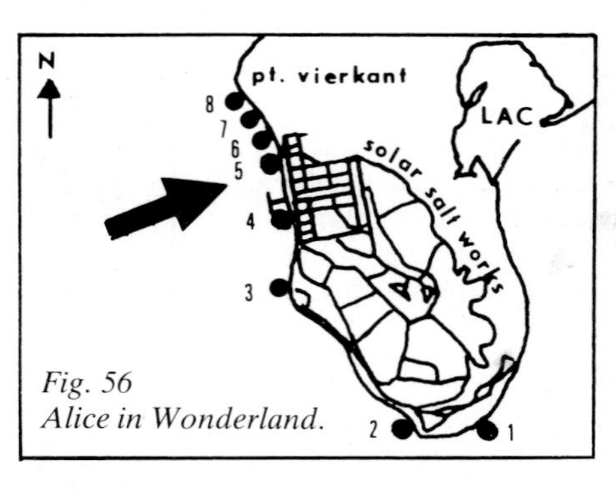


*Fig. 56*
*Alice in Wonderland.*

1 *Boat dive or shore dive*
2 *double barrel mooring/ 4 m (13 ft)*
3 *easy*
4 *100 m (330 ft)*
5 *all levels*
6 *7-9 m (23-30 ft)*
7 *fairly low (reef slope) to fairly high (second reef)*
8 *either one (see reef map)*
9 *27 m (90 ft)*
10 *limited snorkeling value.*

*Fig. 57*
*Southern Stingray.*

reach the 2nd reef, the channel is at 30 m (100 ft) and the top of the reef at 21-24 m (70-80 ft) (fig. 58). The 2nd reef has a rather high coral cover and a great diversity of coral species (a.o. Giant Brain Coral, Mountainous Star Coral, Leaf Coral, Fungus Coral, Flower Coral and Cavernous Star Coral). There are few gorgonians and black corals. Further out is a second drop-off and a gentle reef slope, which is too deep for common safe exploration with SCUBA. *Fishes* that you'll see on the second reef include many Yellowmouth- and Tiger Groupers, the less common Nassau Grouper and sometimes a school of Horse-eye Jacks in the blue water above the reef itself.

On the *shallow terrace* you'll notice extensive fields of Staghorn Coral, that go all the way down to the drop-off zone. In between and under the Staghorn Coral are small heads of smooth Starlet Coral, brain corals and Mountainous Star Coral. The shallow Elkhorn Coral is almost completely lacking in this area. Lots of crustaceans live on this terrace: Arrow Crabs hiding under Longspined Sea Urchins, an occasional Spiny or Slipper Lobster and Banded Coral Shrimp under ledges, showing their location with their white antennae.

*Fig. 58*
*Reef map of the Alice in Wonderland double reef complex. 'Black Margate country' (see Angel City) is in the northern part of the map.*

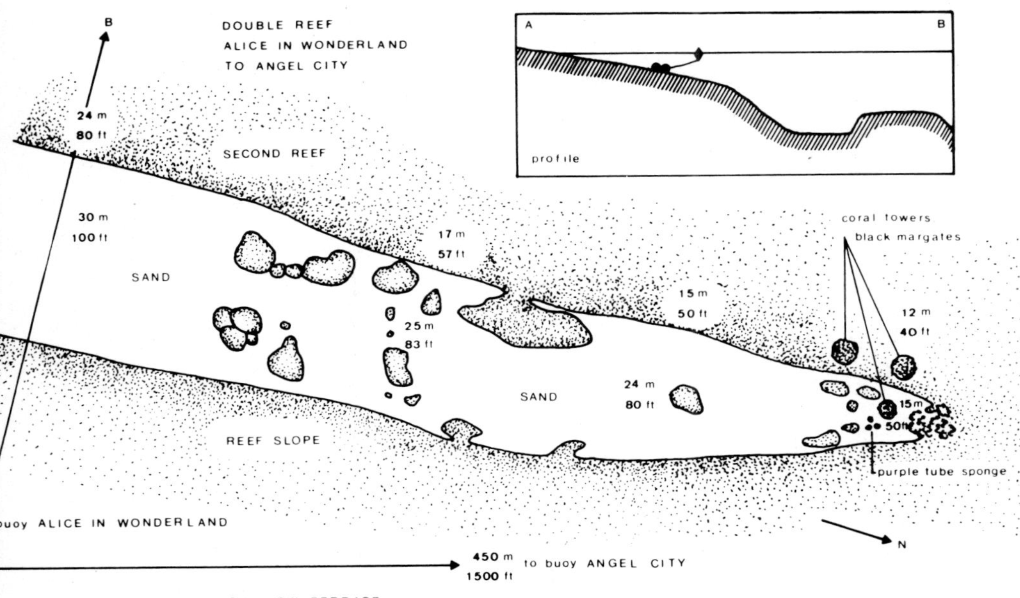

# Dive site:
# **Angel City**

*Fig. 59*
*Eroded tower of Mountainous Star Coral. In the foreground a Do-not-touch-me Sponge.*

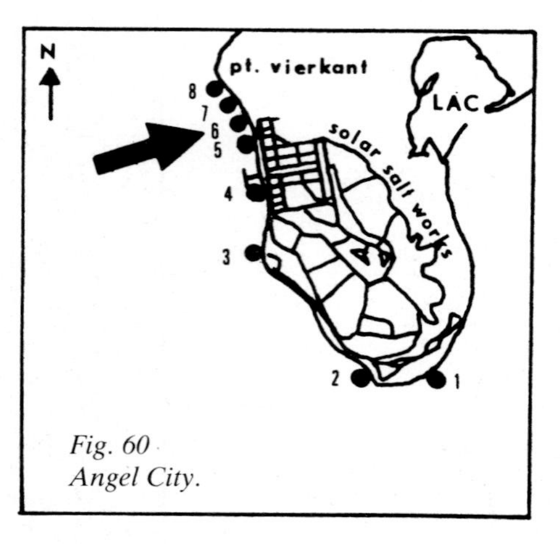


*Fig. 60*
*Angel City.*

1 *Boat dive or shore dive*
2 *double barrel mooring / 6 m (20 ft)*
3 *easy*
4 *80 m (270 ft)*
5 *all levels*
6 *9-10 m (30-33 ft)*
7 *fairly high (second reef)*
8 *south (left, facing the sea); see reef maps*
9 *18 m (60 ft)*
10 *limited snorkeling value.*

**Description**
This is the most popular and most shallow site of the Alice in Wonderland double reef complex. By car you drive south from town to the entrance of the Trans World Radio (TWR) transmitting station. Just before the TWR entrance a track leads you down to the shore. You enter opposite the Angel City buoy that is clearly visible from the shore. Don't forget to take along your waterresistant reef maps.

From the mooring you swim down a gentle *reef slope* that has numerous gorgonians and big boulders of Mountainous Star Coral. You reach a sand channel that separates the reef slope from the second reef and is only a few meters wide here, at 18 m (60 ft).

The face of the *second reef* is at 12 to 15 m (40-50 ft).
By all means swim south (left, facing the sea), for you are heading towards 'Black Margate country'. Keep the sand channel to your left, observe how the second reef almost merges with the slope of the first reef and pretty soon you will see some lobate boulders and temple-like structures of Mountainous Star Coral, in colors of green and tan. The second reef reaches its most shallow point here (9 m - 30 ft). You have arrived. There is no need to swim, find a convenient spot, stay where you are and watch. You will see all the fish cruising by or coming right at you. Over a hundred Black Margates are at home here and cruise slowly from one coral boulder to the other, leaving their hiding places in the crevices underneath those boulders. Most boulders are cleaning stations where you can watch jacks stopping by for a treatment by juvenile Spanish Hogfish. Big Tiger Groupers also call at the cleaning stations. You will see Grey Snappers, Mahogany Snappers, abundant Sergeant Majors that nest in the excavated coral heads and maybe a Yellowfin Grouper. A school of hundreds of snappers moves slowly in the ghostly blue over the seaward edge of the second reef. And in the middle of the sand channel stands a large Purple Tube Sponge

*Fig. 61*
*Black Margates.*

*Fig. 62*
*Black Margates cruising in between the large coral towers.*

*Fig. 63*
*A school of snappers over the second reef.*

like a lonely statue on a pedestal of coral (fig. 58).

Return along the drop-off of the inner reef and you will have seen the best of Angel City. Along this shoulder are many Coneys and Graysbys on the bottom, grazing parrotfish and Blue Tangs along the reef, and schools of chromis and Creole Wrasses in the blue water. And, of course, Yellowtail Snappers, that will examine every diver for possible handouts.

# Dive site:
# **The Lake**

*Fig. 64*
*Two-meter (7 ft) high coral mound in the sand channel at The Lake.*

**Description**
This site is part of the Alice in Wonderland double reef complex. The second reef is separated from the reef slope by a narrow sand channel (about 10 m wide).
The *upper reef slope* is characterized by abundant gorgonians. The lower edge of the reef slope (the beginning of the sand channel) is at 21 m (70 ft). The second reef is clearly visible from this edge. Straight down from the mooring is a 'bridge' of coral heads connecting both reefs. On the shore-side of the channel is a huge coral head, some 4 m (13 ft) across and 2 m (7 ft) tall, consisting basically of Mountainous Star Coral, but with numerous other coral species growing on it as well.

The top of the *second reef* is at 18 m (60 ft) there. The many large 'towers' or 'temples' of Mountainous Star Coral create considerable relief. After some 5-10 min. to the south you arrive at a huge coral tower (Mountainous Star Coral) with a beautiful Purple Tube Sponge next to it.

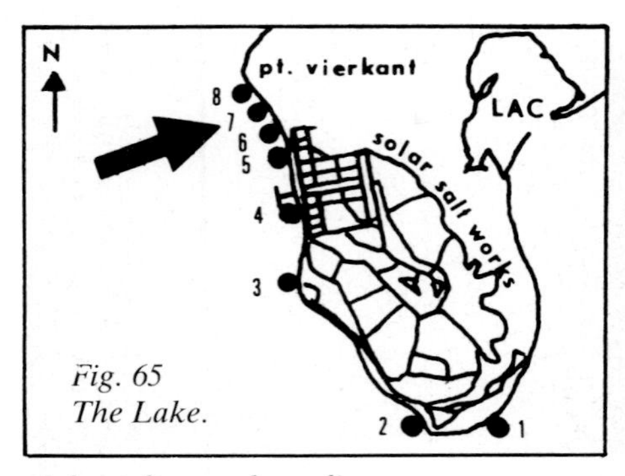


*Fig. 65*
*The Lake.*

1 *boat dive or shore dive*
2 *double barrel mooring / 9 m (30 ft)*
3 *easy*
4 *all levels*
5 *100 m (330 ft)*
6 *9 m (30 ft)*
7 *fairly low (reef slope) to fairly high (2nd reef)*
8 *south (left, facing the sea); see reef map*
9 *21 m (70 ft)*
10 *limited snorkeling value.*

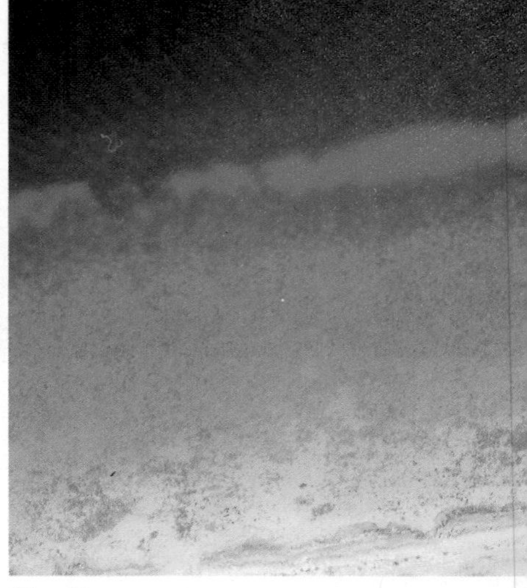

*Fig. 66*
*Aerial photograph of the double reef at The Lake, showing the coral 'bridge' near the mooring (left) and the bridge in between The Lake and Punt Vierkant (right).*

The most common coral species are Mountainous Star Coral, Giant Brain Coral, Flower Coral and Fungus Coral. Few gorgonians and black corals occur. Bridges connect the two reefs in several places as you head south (fig. 70). After about 30 min. you'll see a large colony of the Giant Brain Coral (2 m - 6 ft - across), partly excavated, and then the second reef begins to go down to 20 m (65 ft). This is a good turning point, if you have not turned back already.

The *shallow terrace* is covered with fields of Staghorn Coral along with some Yellow Pencil Coral. From about 4 m (13 ft) up to the shore you'll find almost exclusively sand and coral rubble.

*Fish life* includes a variety of groupers (Yellowmouth Grouper, many Graysbys, Coneys, Rock Hinds and Red Hinds, Nassau Groupers), some Black Margates and numerous Schoolmasters. Yellowtail Snappers are in abundance here, confidently investigating each diver for signs of food. Spotted Moray Eels peek shyly from under coral formations on the shallow slope as well as the second reef area.

*Fig. 67*
*Soapfish resting in large orange sponge.*

# Dive site:
# **Punt Vierkant**

*Fig. 68*
*Yellow Goatfish sheltering near a soft coral (False Plexaura).*

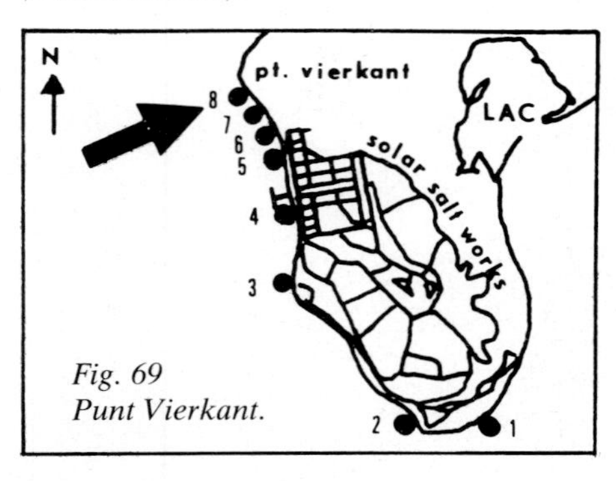


*Fig. 69*
*Punt Vierkant.*

1 *Boat dive or shore dive*
2 *double barrel mooring / 6 m (20 ft)*
3 *easy*
4 *100 m (330 ft)*
5 *all levels*
6 *9-12 m (30-40 ft)*
7 *moderate (reef slope) to high (second reef)*
8 *south (left, facing the sea; see reef map)*
9 *27 m (90 ft)*
10 *limited snorkeling value.*

**Description**
This site is situated at the northern end of the Alice in Wonderland double reef complex. To get here by car you drive south from town, past the Belnem residential area where the road moves off the shore, until the road moves closer to the shore again. Pt. Vierkant is the first buoy past the small lighthouse. Take along your waterresistant reef map.

From the mooring down to the *drop-off* there is a mixed gorgonian-Staghorn Coral community merging into a mixed gorgonian-Mountainous Star Coral community and becoming more lush towards the drop-off.

On the *reef slope* gorgonians and sponges are abundant. The second reef is visible from the lower edge of the reef slope at 27 m (90 ft) where the sand 'lake' begins. Cross the sand channel and swim south (left, facing the sea) over the *second reef*. Initially coral cover on the second reef is not so high, but there are quite a few gorgonians and sponges.

*Fig. 70*
*Reef map of the double reef between Punt Vierkant and Angel City.*

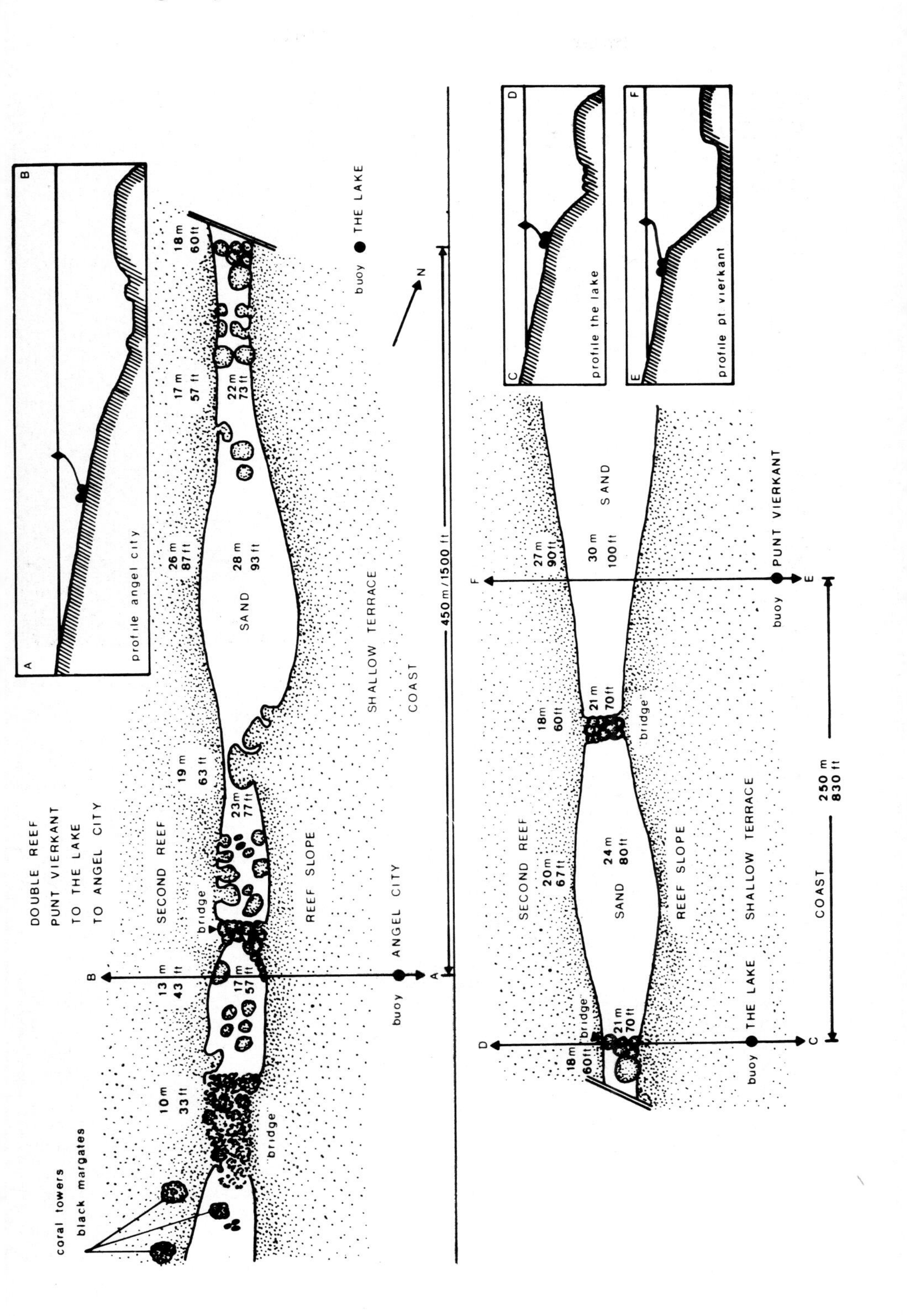

*Fig. 71*
*'Smoking' sponge: an exceptional shot of sperm release by this Purple Tube Sponge.*

*Fig. 72*
*Hawksbill Turtle, not common but widely distributed.*

Towards the south the reef moves up to 18 m (60 ft) and the sand lake narrows (fig. 70). Coral cover becomes higher and the number of gorgonians decreases. The Mountainous Star Coral has developed into towers and the Giant Brain Coral reaches large dimensions. At this point the two reefs are connected by a coral 'bridge' in the channel. If you continue to go south you will reach a second bridge, with a 4 m (13 ft) diameter coral head at 21 m (70 ft), indicating that you have arrived at the mooring of the Lake.

*Fish life.* The sand lake is the habitat of the Garden Eel, Palometa and Southern Stingray. Goatfish and an occasional trunkfish forage here, too.

On the second reef you will see jacks, scad, Schoolmasters and Yellowmouth- and Nassau Groupers. Yellowtail Snappers swim along on your dive; their increasing number and behavior will tell you when you are approaching The Lake.

# Dive site:
# **Windsock Steep**

*Fig. 73*
*Sponge and Butterprint Brain Coral.*

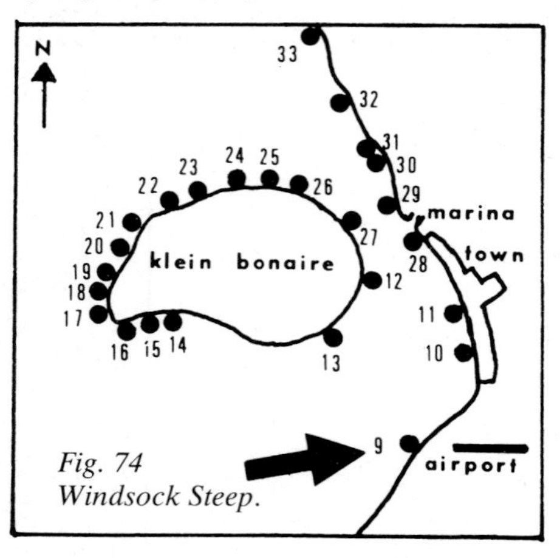


*Fig. 74*
*Windsock Steep.*

1 *Boat or shore dive*
2 *double barrel mooring / 4 m (13 ft)*
3 *easy*
4 *60 m (200 ft)*
5 *all levels*
6 *6-8 m (20-27 ft)*
7 *fairly high*
8 *either way*
9 *21 m (70 ft)*
10 *good snorkeling value.*

**Description**
This site is situated in front of a small sand beach opposite the runway of the airport. It is a popular place for snorkeling close to town.

The *reef slope* is typical and attractive, decorated with gorgonians and sponges. It is a very pleasant and relaxed dive, an excellent first dive to get introduced to Bonaire's reefs.

The *shallow terrace* has some patches of Elkhorn- and fire coral and Staghorn Coral further out towards the drop-off. The drop-off zone is sandy.

*Fish life* includes quite a variety of fish. First of all, in the blue water, there always appear to be some Barracuda here (up to 1.20 m - 4 ft - in length). There is absolutely no reason to be afraid of Barracuda. Furthermore you can see Ocean Triggerfish, many Tiger Groupers, Yellowmouth Groupers and many Sergeant Majors guarding their nests.
Closer to the reef itself look for Schoolmasters, sometimes a Nassau Grouper, Rock Hinds, Queen and French Angelfish, Bluestriped Grunt, Cesar Grunt and Mahogany Snappers. Moray Eels may peek from crevices in the coral. Surgeonfish and goatfish graze in the Staghorn Coral. Smallmouth Grunts school at the edge of the Staghorn Coral patches.

*Fig. 75*
*Barracuda.*

*Fig. 76*
*Tiger Grouper in characteristic striped pattern under a Purple Tube Sponge.*

# Dive site:
# **Calabas Reef**

*Fig. 77*
*The wreck at Calabas Reef.*

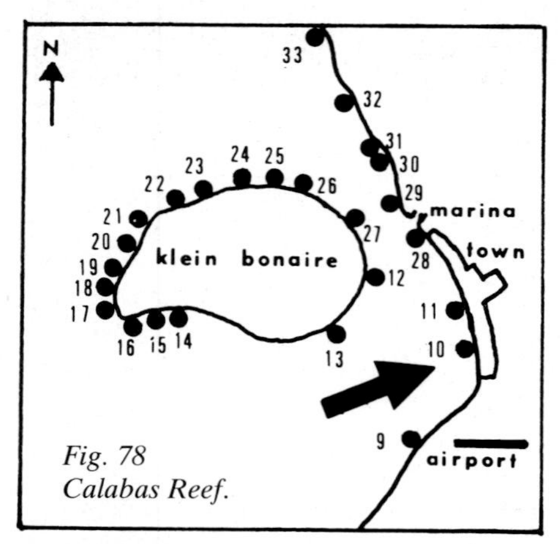


*Fig. 78*
*Calabas Reef.*

1 *Shore dive*
2 —
3 *very easy*
4 *60 m (200 ft)*
5 *all levels*
6 *10-12 m (33-40 ft)*
7 *fairly high*
8 *north (right, facing the sea)*
9 *21 m (70 ft)*
10 *limited snorkeling value, except at Calabas pier.*

**Description**
Located off the Flamingo Beach Hotel is Calabas Reef, Bonaire's most frequently dived site according to the dive statistics. All divers staying at the hotel and/or diving with Dive Bonaire will make their warm-up dive here, do much of their night-diving here or make beach dives in between reef trips at this site. The Dive Bonaire dock or the hotel dock next to the pooldeck offers a convenient entry.

*Shallow terrace.* You swim out over a sand/rubble area towards the drop-off. At 8 m (27 ft) you pass the Dive Bonaire moorings, some of which are made of old anchors. Before you reach the drop-off you will find some gorgonians and small heads of Mountainous Star Coral.

The *reef slope* straight down from the Dive Bonaire dock is quite attractive. You will see a variety of corals, among others large colonies of Giant Brain Coral and quite a few Cavernous Star Corals. Sponges are fairly abundant. Going north (right, facing the sea) you will notice that the slope becomes increasingly less attractive. This is most likely the result of frequent anchoring by yachts. A heavy mooring chain has almost completely destroyed the corals in a strip of 20 m (70 ft) wide. There is also a lot of garbage in this area. Still further north, just north of the Calabas Restaurant pier, at 18 m (60 ft), is the wreck of an aluminum boat, sunk by Captain Don Stewart while he was manager of the former Flamingo Beach Club. There are Christmas Tree Worms, sponges and fire coral growing on the hull. The northernmost of the moorings in front of the hotel is a beautifully overgrown, 3 m (10 ft) long, old anchor at 8 m (27 ft) depth. You are now well north of the Calabas restaurant pier and this is a good point to turn or head into shallow water. At the tip of the Calabas pier you will see lots of Long-spined Sea Urchins and schools of French and Smallmouth Grunt. On the pier itself grows Encrusting Stinging Coral and Orange Tube Coral. This is the best snorkeling spot of Calabas Reef.

*Fig. 79*
*Aerial photograph of Calabas Reef off the Flamingo Beach Hotel.*

Swimming back over the sandy area towards the Dive Bonaire dock you will see many Pink-tipped Anemones with their symbiotic shrimps and juvenile Bluehead Wrasses seeking refuge between the tentacles.

*Fish life* is abundant in the shallow area: there are Mullets, goatfish, French Angelfish from juvenile to adult, lots of grazing fishes like parrotfish and surgeonfish, Spanish Hogfish, Bicolor Damselfish, and, of course the inevitable ever-following Yellowtail Snappers that seem bigger here than anywhere else.

Spotted Moray Eels, a few Goldentail Morays and an occasional Chain Moray are seen on Calabas Reef, along with the Sharptail and Goldspotted Snake Eel. The latter two are frequently mistaken for sea snakes but are actually gentle burrowing crustacean-eaters.

Calabas Reef is an interesting dive at twilight, too. Schooling behavior of the grunts can be seen near the Dive Bonaire dock.

An occasional Octopus poses on a coral head. The eels - both Spotted Morays and snake eels - are out hunting. Even the Orange Tube Coral under Dive Bonaire's dock is beginning to open up and welcome the darkness.

*Fig. 80*
*Mooring north of the Calabas restaurant pier.*

*Fig. 81*
*Schooling Smallmouth Grunts.*

# Dive site:
# **Town Pier**

*Fig. 82*
*Linda Kowalsky photographs sponges and Orange Tube Coral on one of the pillars at Town Pier.*

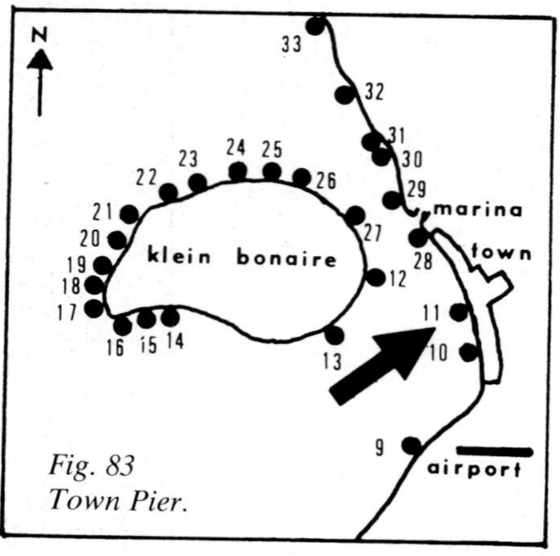


*Fig. 83*
*Town Pier.*

1 *shore dive;* permission required
2 —
3 *easy*
4 —
5 *all levels*
6 *10-12 m (33-40 ft)*
7 *very low*
8 *under the pier*
9 *9 m (30 ft)*
10 *good snorkeling value.*

**Description**

A rather unusual, yet popular site, in particular for night dives. Town pier refers to the 'old pier', that is the pier in the center of town, located in between the customs office and the fish market. For safety reasons the diving here is subject to permission from the harbormaster. Big tugboats are berthed alongside the pier, and their movements along with other ship's movements can seriously endanger divers under the pier. So check with the Harbormasters office (the old fort with the cannon next to the main government building) during the day. Permission will normally be granted if no ships movements are expected during the time span of your dive. Then double-check with the tugboat captain on duty prior to entering the water. When he gives you the final OK you can safely enjoy your dive at the town pier.

The main attraction of diving here is the rich invertebrate life on the pillars of the pier and the abundance of fish sheltering underneath or close to the pier. It is a real dorado for close-up and macrophotography. The pillars are covered with corals (notably Butterprint Brain Coral), encrusting sponges in orange, green and purple, Purple Tube Sponges, bright yellow sponges, Do-not-touch-me Sponges, Christmas Tree Worms, encrusting coralline algae, Orange Tube Coral and lots of Arrow Crabs. Next to the pillars you are also likely to see a Sergeant Major, nervously guarding his nest. Other common fishes on the pillars include the Redlip Blenny and the Redspotted Hawkfish.

In less than 1 m (3 ft) of water, hiding under the shore-end of the pier are thousands of juvenile French Grunts, schools of juvenile and adult Smallmouth Grunts and juvenile silvery fish. Needlefish are swimming with short strokes just below the surface. In addition you will see Mahogany Snapper, Queen Angelfish, French Angelfish ranging from tiny yellowbanded juveniles to adults of 30 cm (1 ft) or more, juvenile Spotted Drum, lots of damselfish

*Fig. 84*
*Interesting possibilities for available light photography at Town Pier.*

and chromis. There are Smooth Trunkfish, Honeycomb Cowfish, Trumpetfish, Blackbar Solderfish, Blue Tangs, Ocean Surgeons, Doctorfish, Barracuda, and, over the sandy bottom, Yellowfin Mojarras and Yellow Goatfish.
Especially when schools of baitfish are nearby Tarpon and some jacks will be seen cruising under the pier.

Aside from the opportunities for close-up photography the mysterious atmosphere, created by the large pillars and the boats casting their ominous shadows over you, invites to available light photography, especially interesting during the late afternoon with a low sun angle.

# Dive site:
# **Just-a-nice-dive** (Kanal)

*Fig. 85*
*Sheet Corals, Mountainous Star Coral and Black Wire Coral on the lower reef slope.*

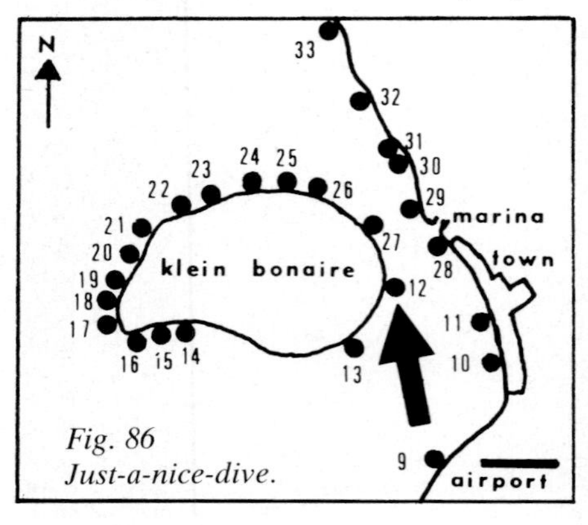


*Fig. 86*
*Just-a-nice-dive.*

1 *Boat dive*
2 *concrete tiles / 25 m (83 ft)*
3 *n.a.*
4 *n.a.*
5 *all levels*
6 *1-2 m (3-7 ft)*
7 *high (on buttresses)*
8 *south (right, facing the sea)*
9 *24 m (80 ft)*
10 *fair snorkeling value.*

**Description**
Like Ebo's Reef, the drop-off at this site is very shallow.
Because of its location in the lee of Kralendijk harbor, this area is littered with bottles that drifted across from town to Klein Bonaire and eventually sank on the reef. Even bottles a hundred years old can still be found here.

The *reef slope* is a system of buttresses and valleys, much like Ebo's Reef, but black coral is far less abundant (few large colonies). The Mountainous Star Coral is not, as usual, the dominant species on the upper reef slope: instead, Yellow Pencil Coral, Club Finger Coral and Leaf Coral are common here.
The buttresses show considerable relief. Large orange sponges are quite abundant. Towards the north, (left, facing the sea) the buttresses gradually disappear and coral cover becomes lower (more sand on the reef slope). Sponges remain abundant and black corals tend to be larger.

*Fig. 87*
*Bottle graveyard.*

*Fig. 89*
*Ocean Triggerfish.*

On the *shallow terrace* you will see scattered Elkhorn Coral, patches of Staghorn Coral, small heads of brain coral and gorgonians. Especially the Black Sea Rod is abundant. Grazing fish like parrotfish and Blue Tangs are abundant here.

*Fish life.* As this dive site is not being dived frequently, the Yellowtail Snappers have not yet become a nuisance. There are some big Tiger Groupers, White-spotted Filefish, and an Ocean Triggerfish is often seen here. Abundant fish life is seen in the drop-off zone and upper slope: Yellow Goatfish, Sergeant Majors, Mahogany Snappers are all common and at the drop-off is a small school of Bermuda Chubs.

*Fig. 88*
*Bottle overgrown by Encrusting Stinging Coral. On top a colony of Leaf Coral.*

# Dive site:
# **Nearest Point** (Piedra Kolet)

*Fig. 90*
*Dee Scarr in characteristic pose: can of fishfood in one hand, one of 'her' pet Morays, The Prince, in the other.*

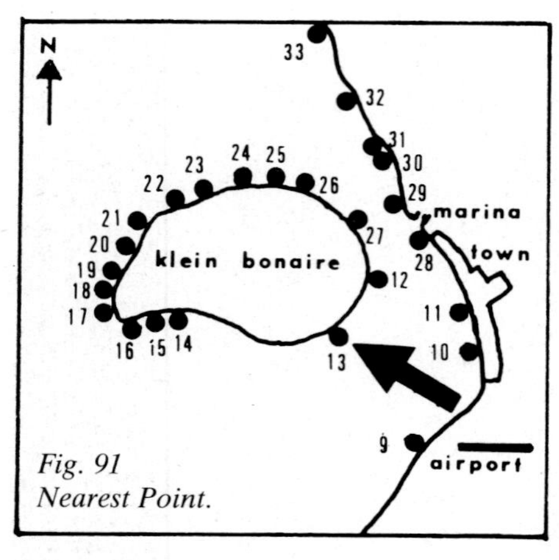


*Fig. 91*
*Nearest Point.*

1 *boat dive*
2 *double barrel mooring / 7 m (23 ft)*
3 *n.a.*
4 *n.a.*
5 *all levels*
6 *6-9 m (20-30 ft)*
7 *fairly high*
8 *either way*
9 *24-27 m (80-90 ft)*

**Description**
This site was moored in 1981, but apparently at the time of publication of this guide it has not been dived frequently.
It is about the 'nearest point' of Klein Bonaire seen from the Flamingo Beach Hotel.

The *drop-off zone* is sandy, but otherwise characterized by the presence of gorgonians, Mountainous Star Coral, Smooth Starlet Coral and Giant Brain Coral. Mortality among the corals is fairly high. Among the gorgonians that are abundant downslope to 9 m (30 ft) particularly the Black Sea Rod is conspicuous. This species created a lot of interest in the pharmaceutical industry because of its high content in prostaglandins.
These soft and hard corals form a ledge running parallel to the coastline of Klein Bonaire, a kind of sea garden that is at a good depth for exploration during your return to the boat.

On the *upper reef slope* you will see much Flower Coral and patches of Yellow Pencil Coral. Some big orange sponges and Purple Tube Sponges can also be found here.

On the *lower reef slope* some good-sized black coral is present. There is a Sheet Coral/Mountainous Star Coral roof shingle community too, with some extensive untouched areas of Sheet and Scroll Coral at about 30-39 m (100-130 ft).
The reef is a system of fairly well-developed buttresses and valleys.

The *shallow terrace* from 3 m (10 ft) up is rather barren of coral, sandy with staghorn rubble and some gorgonians. Because of the location of Nearest Point in relation to Bonaire, this dive site (like Just-a-Nice-Dive) is likely to conceal some old bottles in the shallows.

*Fish life.* Since fish have not been fed indiscriminately here, the Yellowtail Snappers are still controllable. You are likely to see a few big groupers on the reef slope, and one or two Spotted Moray Eels.
On the upper reef slope and the shallow

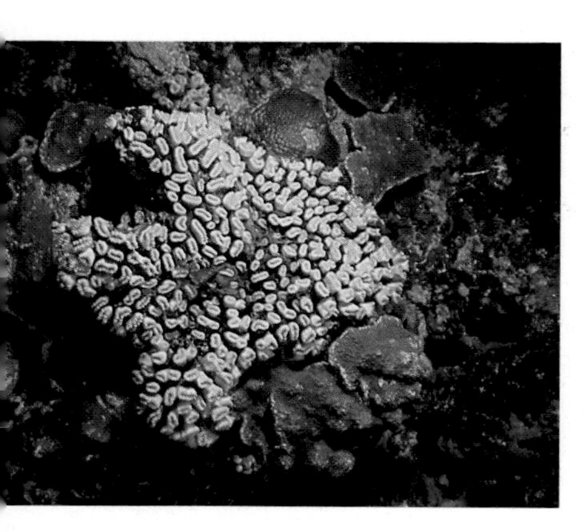

*Fig. 92*
*Flower Coral.*

terrace of Nearest Point you are likely to see a small school of Palometa cruising about in midwater. Palometas are silvery fish with faint vertical dark stripes, and extended dark dorsal and ventral fins. They will school near a diver - especially someone wearing white fins - and soon learn to take bread or cheese directly from a diver's hand.

*Fig. 93*
*One of the species of Sheet Coral* (Agaricia grahamae).

# Dive site: **South Bay**

*Fig. 94*
*'Elmer and the Eel'.*

*Fig. 96*
*Club Finger Coral.*

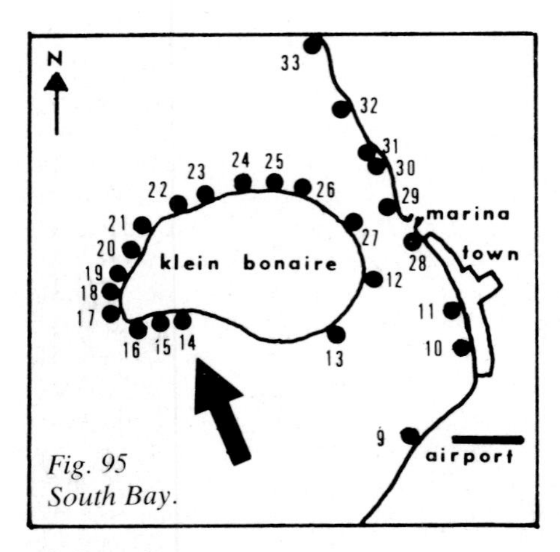


*Fig. 95*
*South Bay.*

1 *Boat dive*
2 *engine block / 5 m (17 ft)*
3 *n.a.*
4 *n.a.*
5 *all levels*
6 *10-12 m (33-40 ft)*
7 *high*
8 *either way*
9 *24-27 m (80-90 ft)*
10 *good snorkeling value when sea is calm*

**Description**
This site is situated on the exposed side of Klein Bonaire.
A light to moderate chop is to be expected.

On the *upper reef slope* the Club Finger Coral, Yellow Pencil Coral and Flower Coral are quite common. They often are settled on the skeletons of partly dead Mountainous Star Corals that rise above the reef surface. Gorgonians are rather abundant and you will also find black corals, although clearly fewer than at nearby Forest (ref. no. 16).

The *lower reef slope* is covered extensively with Sheet Corals. If you swim east (to the left, facing the sea) you will not find buttresses until after some 30 min., when a fairly deep sand valley appears. Towards the west (right) are some very pronounced buttresses and valleys and a couple of small vertical walls, either formed by an outward growth of the reef from the drop-off or representing the remains of a cliff developed during a past, lower, sea level. The first wall is just west of the mooring at 13 m (43 ft), going down to

*Fig. 97*
*Old anchor at South Bay.*

17 m (57 ft). A bit further to the west is a ledge from 12 to 14 m (40 to 47 ft) and next a third, less pronounced wall at 12 m (40 ft) down to 15 m (50 ft).
Continuing to the west you have three buttresses jutting out from the reef and alternating sand valleys testifying to some fairly recent reef slides. Look for an old anchor at 13 m (43 ft), past the third buttress and just east of a wide sand valley.

Just like Forest the *shallow terrace* is divided in two by a 'step' at about 4 m (13 ft). Lush gorgonians and scattered, small heads of Mountainous Star Coral characterize the lower terrace. The upper part is a hardrock plateau, covered with gorgonians and small heads of Smooth Starlet Coral and brain corals.

*Fish life.* Expect to see some big Tiger Groupers, perhaps a Yellowfin Grouper, Horse-eye Jacks and big Schoolmasters. The Yellowtail Snappers will be present as usual.
The first wall is the home of Benedict Arnold, Bonaire's first 'personality' Spotted Moray Eel. Beginning his (in)famous career by wrapping himself around the neck of Elmer Munk in November of 1980, this 1 m (3,5 ft) eel wrapped himself around several divers but could not get into print (Skin Diver, May 1981) until he nipped Paul Tzimoulis, editor-publisher of *Skin Diver Magazine,* on the hand as Tzimoulis was trying to feed him.
Now, more than a year later, Benedict still waits for divers to feed him - but he only gets 'frisky' if there is a smell of fish in the water. (Forewarned is forearmed, divers!) Don't feed fish to the fish on South Bay.

# Dive site:
# **Hands Off**

Fig. 98
*Bonairean dive guides Cedric Angela and Chano Thielman wrestle a camera away from disobedient diver.*

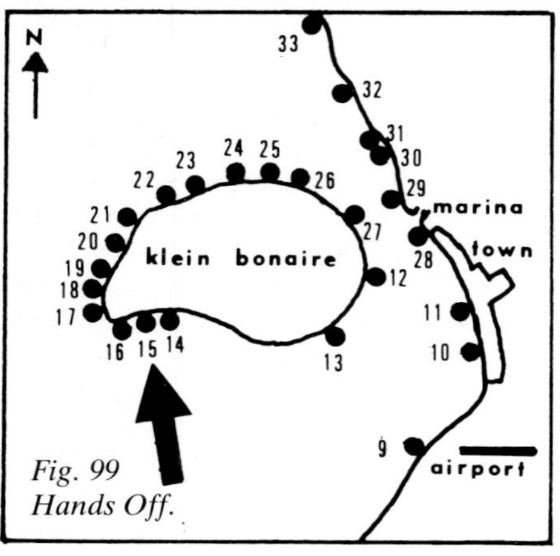


*Fig. 99*
*Hands Off.*

1 *Boat dive*
2 *double barrel mooring / 6 m (20 ft)*
3 *n.a.*
4 *n.a.*
5 *experienced, non-camera carrying divers only (see below)*
6 *8 m (27 ft)*
7 *high (on the buttresses)*
8 *east (left, facing the sea)*
9 *24-27 m (80-90 ft)*
10 *limited snorkeling value*

**Description**
This site was opened and moored in 1981 to conduct an experiment. Many believe that inexperienced and camera-carrying divers do relatively more damage to the corals than others.
The first category because they are not yet able to conrol their movements well, the second because their attention is absorbed by the subject they want to record. To test the validity of this assumption we needed a dive site where resort course and novice divers as well as camera-carrying divers would not be allowed, and that was comparable to an area where those divers would have unlimited access. We selected a site east of Forest, on the basis of its similarity with Forest, named it 'Hands off' appropriately and selected and marked permanent quadrats for periodical monitoring. Very unfortunately, in July 1981, a storm caused a lot of siltation along the reef slope and complicated the experiment. At the time of publication of this guide it was not yet decided whether or not the experiment would be carried on.

Like Forest the reef is characterized by a system of buttresses and alternating valleys. The buttresses in this area are quite well-developed. Characteristic for Hands off is also the abundant black coral.

The *drop-off* zone is narrow with numerous gorgonians. Straight down from the mooring is a wide sand valley. Some valleys are quite narrow and the neighboring buttresses steep. In some valleys you can see large broken-off and slid-down coral heads: they toppled at the drop-off and caused true 'avalanches'.

The *reef slope,* down to 21 m (70 ft), is the most interesting part: there are big heads of Mountainous Star Coral, Cavernous Star Coral, Giant Brain Coral, a lot of Flower Coral and Yellow Pencil Coral and a variety of sponges. Gorgonians are abundant just below the drop-off zone. Towards the east (left, facing the sea) the reef appears to be less affected by siltation.
Roof shingles of Mountainous Star Coral and Sheet Corals are present from 21-24 m (70-80 ft) down. The roof shingle community was particularly affected by siltation after the storm.

The *shallow terrace* is sandy with some gorgonians and small heads of Mountainous Star Coral. From 5 m (17 ft) up the terrace is covered with staghorn rubble. Some living Staghorn Coral, the Pink-tipped Anemone and many gorgonians occur.

*Fish life.* You can expect some big Tiger Groupers, Yellowmouth Groupers and Rock Hind. Characteristic for the drop-off zone are the Black Durgons. More shallow there may be a school of Bermuda Chubs and big parrotfishes like the Midnight- and Rainbow Parrotfish.

# Dive site:
# **Forest**

*Fig. 100*
*Dichotomous Black Coral.*

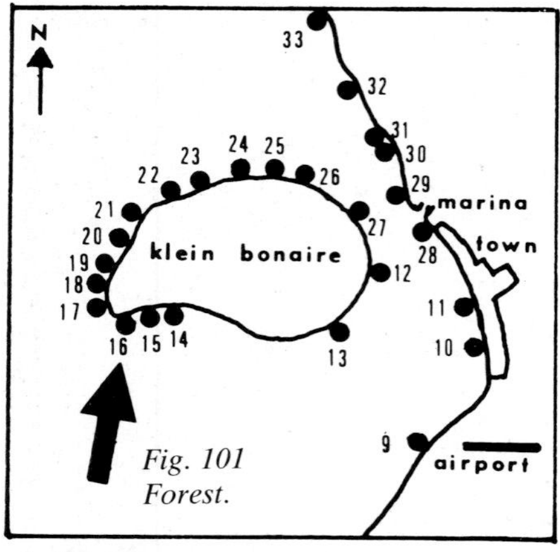


*Fig. 101*
*Forest.*

1 *Boat dive*
2 *double barrel mooring / 7 m (23 ft)*
3 *n.a.*
4 *n.a.*
5 *all levels (except novice divers)*
6 *8-9 m (27-30 ft)*
7 *high (on the buttresses)*
8 *either way (but current usually going west)*
9 *24-27 m (80-90 ft)*
10 *good snorkeling value when sea is calm.*

**Description**
This dive site got its name from the black coral 'forest' that is found here. Another striking feature of this area is the extremely well-developed system of buttresses and valleys.

The drop-off zone has a lush Mountainous Star Coral/gorgonian community. On the *upper reef slope* Mountainous Star Coral is clearly the dominant species; in addition, Flower Coral, Giant Brain Coral, patches of Yellow Pencil Coral, and Club Finger Coral are abundant. Gorgonians are most abundant down to 15 m (50 ft). Sponges are quite common; the large orange sponges are particularly striking. Nice Sheet Corals occur on the *lower reef slope,* below 24 m (80 ft). Straight down from the mooring is a near-vertical buttress, going down to 21 m (70 ft) only, with two caves, one at 27 m (90 ft), the other at 21 m (70 ft) on the Hands-off side of the buttress.
Note that most black coral grows on the crest and the eastern side of the buttresses (direction of the prevailing current is west), whereas gorgonians appear to be more abundant in the valleys. To the east the reef is a continuous system of buttresses.
Towards the west the reef changes remarkably. There are only a few more buttresses, the slope angle slightly decreases, coral cover becomes less and the reef has less relief. Black coral becomes less abundant and gorgonians increase both in number of species and in absolute number. Soon after departing from the mooring site you can see beautiful Deepwater Gorgonians (indication of currents) in about 21-30 m (70-100 ft). Returning after some 30-40 min., just above the drop-off you will see an incredible forest of gorgonians. The gorgonians extend upward to about 6 m (20 ft), where pillar coral is fairly common too.

The *shallow terrace* is divided in an upper and a lower terrace with a 1 m 'step' at 4 m (13 ft). On the lower terrace gorgonians are quite abundant, but from 3 m

*Fig. 103*
*Deepwater Gorgonian.*

*Fig. 102*
*Buttresses and valleys are well-developed at Forest.*

(10 ft) up the terrace is hard rock covered with sand and many loose coral fragments. Around the gorgonians look for hidden tiny filefish; pairs of White-spotted Filefish are often seen on the shallow terrace at Forest.

*Fish life.* The location of this site, near the southern tip of Klein Bonaire, is responsible for occasional currents and for a lot of fish action. You will see big groupers, including some old Tiger Groupers, Schoolmasters, Mahogany Snappers, Bluestriped Grunts, Horse-eye Jacks, Queen- and French Angelfish and, in the drop-off zone, Black Durgons. Also lots of Yellowtail Snappers will follow your every move, hoping for a handout.

A friendly Spotted Moray Eel lives near the cave at 27 m (90 ft).

# Dive site:
# **South-west Corner**

*Fig. 104*
*Iridescent sponges.*

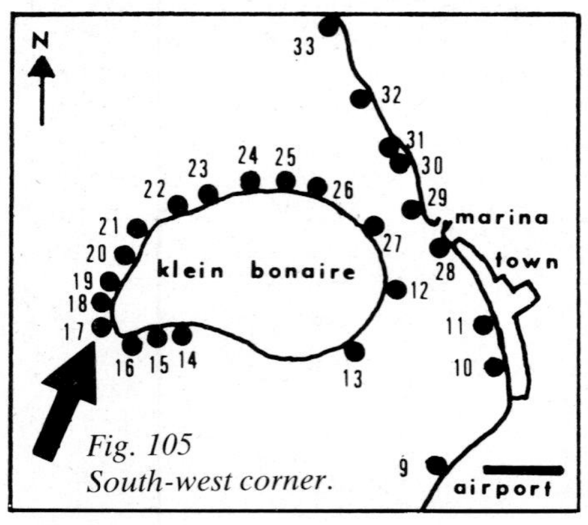


*Fig. 105*
*South-west corner.*

1 *Boat dive*
2 *double barrel mooring / 4 m (13 ft)*
3 *n.a.*
4 *n.a.*
5 *alle levels*
6 *9 m (30 ft)*
7 *fairly high*
8 *south-east (left, facing the sea)*
9 *21-24 m (70-80 ft)*
10 *limited snorkeling value*

**Description**
This is a very popular, colorful and varied dive site at the south-western tip of Klein Bonaire. Occasional strong currents - strong by Bonairean standards - occur here.

Large numbers of gorgonians, especially the Slimy and Dry Sea Plume, occur in the *drop-off* zone. Seaward of the mooring on the drop-off at about 10 m (33 ft) is a Purple Tube Sponge with more than 40 individual tubes. At 15 m (50 ft) is a big coral head (Mountainous Star Coral) the top of which is a cleaning station serviced by juvenile Spanish Hogfish. It also represents a nesting area for the Sergeant Major and in a crevice lives a well-camouflaged bivalve, the Rough Lima (note the tentacle-like extensions of the mantle). At about 17 m (57 ft), just on the Twixt side of the mooring is a spot with 12 separate azure sponges growing close together.

The *reef slope* creates a rich and diverse impression due to the great variety of invertebrates present. Both gorgonians and black corals are well-represented. A variety of sponges adds to the overall colorful aspect of the reef slope. Coral cover is slightly higher south-east of the mooring (direction Forest). There is little coral zonation, but considerable relief, especially on the upper slope and more so towards the south-east, where some really big towers of Mountainous Star Coral and big heads of Giant Brain Coral can be seen. Towards the south-east the relief of the reef increases and so does the number of gorgonians. To the north-west (direction Twixt) the number of black corals increases.

A bit south-east (left) of the mooring, at 22 m (73 ft) is a nice old anchor with four flukes, just below a large orange sponge. The reef slope ends abruptly at a depth of 36 m (120 ft) and is followed by a fairly flat sand/rubble terrace.

*Shallow terrace.* Between 7 and 4 m (23 and 13 ft) is a mixed Staghorn/Mountainous Star Coral community with abundant gorgonians (Slimy and Dry Sea Plumes

*Fig. 106*
*Aerial photograph of South-west Corner showing the elkhorn and staghorn zone.*

*Fig. 107*
*Old anchor at South-west Corner.*

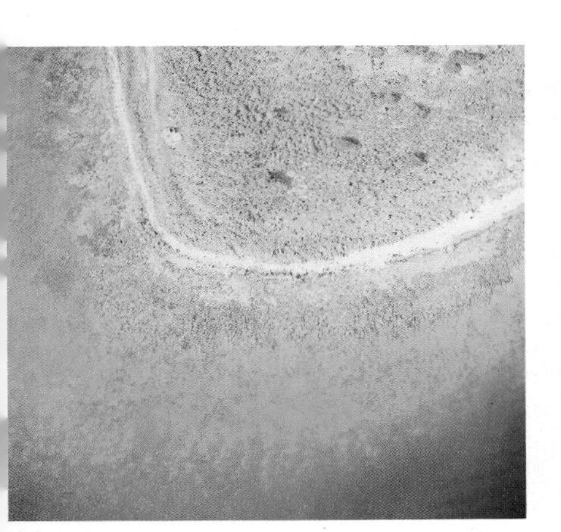

*Fig. 108*
*Common Lettuce Slug.*

and some Common Sea Fans). The 'bird's nest'-like tangle in the gorgonians, upon close examination, turns out to be the many-armed Basket Starfish, sleeping the day through. At night this animal untangles its arms and holds them out to filter food from the water. Some of the dead Staghorn Coral is overgrown by a green sponge, some by the Encrusting Gorgonian, other heavily encrusted by pink coralline algae. From 4 m (13 ft) up there are less gorgonians but the Staghorn Coral continues, along with some patches of Elkhorn Coral, and isolated fire coral/Mountainous Star Coral mountains. Among the Staghorn Coral you can find many Pink-tipped Anemones and the Common Lettuce Slug, a shell-less mollusk. It has been given various common names: Ribbon Nudibranch, Lettuce Sea Slug, Ruffleback Nudibranch, even Bonairean Nudibranch. Whatever you choose to call it, you'll find it a charming animal. In length up to almost 10 cm (4 inches), the Common Lettuce Slug lives on algae-covered rock or dead coral. It can often be found on the bases of the dead Staghorn Corals. In pastel colors of green, blue, even lavendar, this animal is an appealing subject for macro-photographers. Photographers who have tried to pose it on living coral or sponges know not to try again: it simply won't attach to coral or sponges. Photo backgrounds which are acceptable to the animals and attractive in the picture are red or green algal mats.
One interesting characteristic of this sea slug is its lack of palatability to fish. If an 'attack' yellowtail zooms up to gobble down the sea slug, the fish either comes to a screeching pre-gobble halt, or spits the slug out instantly (usually unharmed, too).

*Fish life* includes Yellowmouth Groupers, some big Tiger Groupers, White-spotted Filefish, Schoolmasters and, in the drop-off zone Black Durgons and many Sergeant Majors. Bonairean 'attack' Yellowtail Snappers patrol the drop-off here in full force. Occasionally you will see the Ocean Triggerfish, or a large school of Horse-eye Jacks, in the blue water, or a Porgy or a Midnight Parrotfish.

# Dive site:
# **Twixt**

*Fig. 109*
*Heavily eroded coral tower and Yellow Goatfish.*

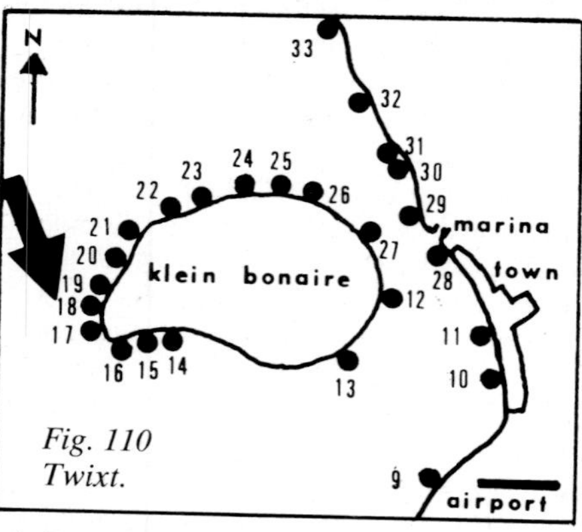


*Fig. 110*
*Twixt.*

1 *Boat dive*
2 *double barrel mooring / 6 m (20 ft)*
3 *n.a.*
4 *n.a.*
5 *all levels*
6 *10-12 m (33-40 ft)*
7 *fairly high*
8 *either way; current usually going south (left, facing the sea) occasionally fairly strong*
9 *24 m (80 ft)*
10 *good snorkeling value.*

**Description**
Similar to Valerie's Hill. Black coral and sponges are abundant.

Coral mortality is rather high in the *drop-off zone*. Many corals are partly covered with algae or Encrusting Gorgonians. In places the drop-off looks a bit barren, but gorgonians are present all along.

The *reef slope* shows no distinct zonation, although some Sheet and Scroll Coral is typical for the lower slope. Black coral and sponges are plentiful, and especially along the upper slope, gorgonians. Look also for crinoids. Just below the drop-off Mountainous Star Corals build towering structures.

The *shallow terrace* is wide and an extensive field of Staghorn Coral stretches from 8 m (27 ft) to about 3 m (10 ft). Interspersed with the Staghorn Coral are fire corals, gorgonians (primarily False Plexaura and Dry or Slimy Sea Plumes), heads of Giant Brain Coral, Mountainous Star Coral, brain corals and Yellow Pencil Coral. From 3 m (10 ft) to the surface you will find the usual Elkhorn Coral, plus

*Fig. 111*
*School of chromis feeding on plankton in the blue water above the drop-off.*

patches of Leafy Stinging Coral and Club Finger Coral.

Both dive directions are quite similar and need not be described separately.

*Fish life* is very plentiful at Twixt. In the blue water along the reef are large schools of chromis and Creole Wrasse.

Frequently, farther out from the reef at depths ranging from about 6 to 21 m (20 to 70 ft) a school of 50-100 Horse-eye Jacks cruises. A diver making no awkward or sudden movements can swim right into this school for an unusual close-up of all those fish.

Along the reef slope fairly large Tiger and Yellowmouth Groupers are common. Immediately seaward of the mooring at about 20 m (65 ft) depth, there is a very obtrusive star coral head, which is a well-established cleaning station. Around it you can see as many as three fish (usually groupers) being cleaned at once, by Neon Gobies, juvenile Spanish Hogfish, and even some shrimp. Take a position along the reef (being careful not to damage the coral) and watch the groupers being cleaned - it's well worth the time. They loll from side to side, opening their mouths, flaring out their gill plates, and generally looking very pleased to be losing their parasites.

The shallow terrace at Twixt is also very lush with life: Spanish Hogfish, Goldentail Morays peeking out of coral heads, Coneys, etc. Trumpetfish seem to be everywhere here. Sometimes you will see 5 or even more Trumpetfish - of all colors: blue, red, yellow, brown - hanging vertically above the bottom, with other reef fish and maybe even a small jack, all moving in a group. Look closely and you'll probably see that they're around a swimming Goldentail or Spotted Moray Eel. The reasons for this behavior are in doubt.

# Dive site:
# **Valerie's Hill**

*Fig. 112*
*Diver Pat Uyeno and Deepwater Gorgonian.*

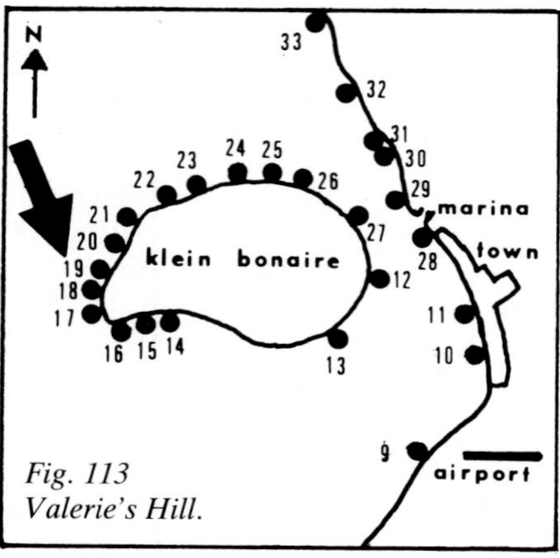


*Fig. 113*
*Valerie's Hill.*

1 *Boat dive*
2 *double barrel mooring / 6 m (20 ft)*
3 *n.a.*
4 *n.a.*
5 *all levels*
6 *9-10 m (30-33 ft)*
7 *high*
8 *either way; current usually going south-west (left, facing the sea)*
9 *24-27 m (80-90 ft)*
10 *good snorkeling value.*

**Description**
This site was named after Captain Don Stewart's wife by local dive guides. It is similar to Twixt. Sponges and black coral are plentiful.

The *drop-off zone* looks rather barren because of a low coral cover and some mortality amongst the corals.
Just past the drop-off and on the *upper reef slope* the Mountainous Star Coral forms large structures, towering above the reef. Sponges are abundant all along the reef slope and you will see many large orange sponges and Purple Tube Sponges. Black coral is also abundant here, but gorgonians are not, apart from the Encrusting Gorgonian.
The *lower reef slope* has Sheet and Scroll Corals and there are many algae in the deep reef (from about 24 m - 80 ft - down).

Both dive directions do not require separate descriptions. After some 10 min. to the north-east (right, facing the sea) is a deep and wide sand valley flanked by two marked buttresses.
Notice that black corals only occur on the north-east side of the buttresses. At about

*Fig. 114*
*Fire coral and Yellow Pencil Coral covering a reef patch destroyed by anchoring.*

21 m (70 ft) in this rubble valley is a huge orange sponge, and at around 16 m (53 ft) a Purple Tube Sponge with wide, long tubes.

The *shallow terrace* is rather barren from 10 to 7 m (33 to 23 ft) with scattered gorgonians. From 7 m (23 ft) up there is a dense field of Staghorn Coral. Elkhorn Coral is found in shallow water (less than 3 m - 10 ft). Anchor damage is visible near the lighthouse: a large patch of Yellow Pencil Coral with fire coral and lots of Bicolor Damselfish just inshore of the mooring looks like an example; the area was probably destroyed by anchoring and subsequently colonized by the Yellow Pencil Coral.

*Fish life.* Large groupers are definitely not unusual here. Like this entire 'facet' of Klein Bonaire (from Twixt to Carl's Hill) the Coneys and Graysbys are very aggressive on Valerie's Hill - but fun to feed. A discriminating fish feeder here can often attract less common fish, such as a Scrawled Filefish or some of the grey parrotfish.

# Dive site:
# **Mi Dushi** (Johanna's Revenge)

*Fig. 115*
*The 'Wagon Wheel' sponge.*

**Description**

The mooring on this site was placed originally for the 'Mi Dushi', a boat that ran one-day charter trips with tourists. The anchor chain of the mooring runs all the way to the drop-off and has knocked off most of the Staghorn Coral, so the mooring area looks pretty barren. There is a small beach with easy entrance to the sea, just in case you want to spend the day here and dive or snorkel from the beach.

In the *drop-off zone* gorgonians (Dry and Slimy Sea Plumes, False Plexaura, Sea Rod and Encrusting Gorgonian) are abundant, but coral cover is low and coral mortality high.

Along the *reef slope* to the south-west (left, facing the sea) you will find well-developed buttresses, some of which are quite steep. Sponges are abundant and varied at Mi Dushi.

On the second buttress to the left of the

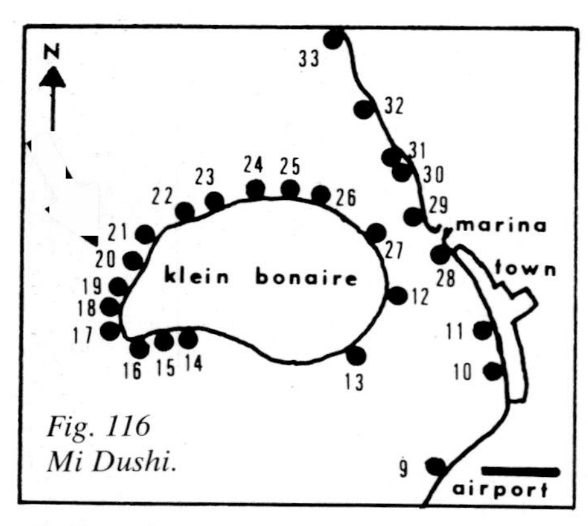


*Fig. 116*
*Mi Dushi.*

1 *Boat dive*
2 *3 barrels connected with a long heavy chain / 5 and 8 m (17 and 27 ft)*
3 *n.a.*
4 *n.a.*
5 *all levels*
6 *10-12 m (33-40 ft)*
7 *fairly high*
8 *either way; current usually going south-west (left, facing the sea)*
9 *24-27 m (80-90 ft)*
10 *fair snorkeling value.*

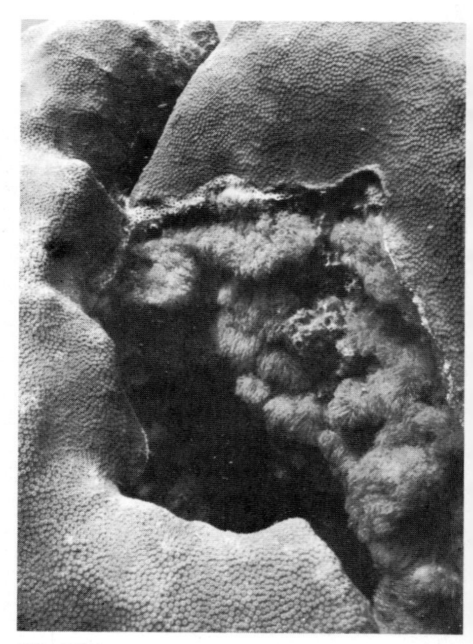

*Fig. 117*
*Dead surface of Mountainous Star Coral overgrown by Encrusting Gorgonian. The long polyps give the gorgonian a fuzzy appearance.*

mooring, at about 18 m (60 ft) is the 'Wagon Wheel' sponge, a Purple Tube Sponge which has grown like half a wagon wheel, with spokes. Gorgonians are present, but not as abundant as in the drop-off zone and there are large black corals on the lower reef slope, to the south-west in particular. Also along the lower reef slope are beautiful Sheet and Scroll Corals. The main differences between south-west and north-east (left and right) are the buttresses and the more abundant black coral towards the south-west.

The *shallow terrace* is wide and for the greater part covered with Staghorn Coral. In between the staghorn you will see Yellow Pencil Coral, Mountainous Star Coral and fire coral. Patches of flat hard rock, partly covered with sand, also occur, with scattered Mustard Hill Coral and Elliptical Star Coral. Close to shore we find a zone with Elkhorn Coral.

*Fish life.* Some big Tiger and Yellowmouth Groupers are found in this area. While wandering around the chain-created 'barren' area at the end of the dive, look closely to see a profusion of life: Bicolor Damselfish darting in and out of the rubble, along with an occasional intense-blue-and-orange Pygmy Angelfish. Redspotted Hawkfish rest among the pieces of rubble. All the small groupers are here, too: Graysbys, Coneys, Rock Hinds and Red Hinds.
Invertebrates around the rubble include Fire Worms, Arrow Crabs, and even an occasional Queen Conch, which are now quite rare on Bonaire.

*Fig. 118*
*Coney.*

# Dive site:
# **Carl's Hill** (Punta P'abou)

*Fig. 119*
*Vertical reef slope with diver Christie Dovale.*

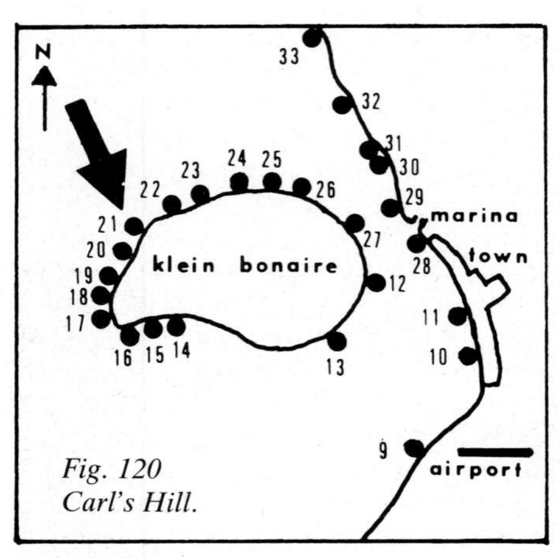


*Fig. 120*
*Carl's Hill.*

1 *Boat dive*
2 *double barrel mooring / 7 m (23 ft)*
3 *n.a.*
4 *n.a.*
5 *all levels*
6 *10 m (33 ft)*
7 *fairly high*
8 *east (to the right, facing the sea)*
9 *21 m (70 ft)*

**Description**
Carl's Hill is a very lush dive site, and due to the nature of the interactions between coral and fish life here, we have discussed them together instead of separating them. Also, there are several ways to dive Carl's Hill - it is certainly not possible to see 'everything' here in one dive!

Carl's Hill, named after underwater photographer Carl Roessler, is famous for its vertical wall just east (to the right) of the mooring. One way to do the dive is to swim east above the drop-off across a lush gorgonian forest, past a fairly prominent buttress and a sand valley, at which point you will see the contours of the wall in the blue. Take plenty of time to explore the wall and then return as you came, shallow The *wall* stretches from 10 to 20 m (33-67 ft) depth. At the upper edge of the wall, at 10 m (33 ft), close to a stand of Pillar Coral, some Tiger Groupers and a big Rock Hind can often be seen. It seems to be a favourite cleaning station and you can approach a Tiger Grouper at this station to within 1.5 m (5 ft). He will

*Fig. 121*
*Cleaning station at the upper edge of the wall, next to Pillar Coral.*

move when you come too close, but will go right back to the same spot when you back off. On the upper part of the wall you will find lots of Cavernous Star Coral in colors from green to purple to red, and Butterprint Brain Coral. There is a variety of sponges on the wall and the colors of the invertebrates in addition to those of the Cavernous Star Coral are exciting. There are orange, green and purple encrusting sponges and crustose coralline algae in pink and purple. Black corals, especially Black Wire Coral, are also present on the wall.

Typical for the deep reef and for walls is a flattened or encrusting growth form of corals. The deepest part of the wall has some flat Sheet Corals.

The *shallow terrace* straight up from the wall is more narrow than anywhere else on Klein Bonaire. On the terrace are some gorgonians, fire corals and brain corals followed by beautifully developed Elkhorn Coral closer to the shore. Swimming back to the mooring you pass over a field of Staghorn Coral from 6 m (20 ft) up or a gorgonian forest, consisting mainly of sea plumes, if you swim deeper than 6 m (20 ft). If you look carefully into the sea plumes you are likely to see a tangle that looks almost like a bird's nest: the filter-feeding, nocturnal Basket Starfish, all curled up for its daytime rest. Just below the mooring you will see two golden Coneys that are not at all shy and will take food from your hands. The mooring area is also very good for snorkeling with lush growth of Elkhorn Coral and upright plates of Leafy Stinging Coral in the shallow part. Shoreward of the mooring the Elkhorn Coral forms deep ledges, almost caves, in which Porcupine Fish can often be seen peeking out at divers.

There are several resident Spotted Moray Eels at Carl's Hill; they have to be fast when divers feed them, because if Percival the Pudding Wife doesn't steal their fish, a large Rock Hind or greedy Coney will.

The *reef slope* at Carl's Hill is very beautiful too, and another way to plan your dive is to swim along the reef slope, at 15-21 m (50-70 ft), until you come around the

*Fig. 122*
*Cavernous Star Coral is abundant on vertical slopes.*

buttress, through a cloud of Blue Chromis, and see the vertical wall.
As the reef slopes down, the soft corals become more and more sparse and the number of stony corals increases. Cleaning stations are common - you will frequently see a grouper hovering over a rounded brain coral head just below the boat, at about 20 m (70 ft), being cleaned by industrious Neon Gobies.
Between the mooring and the vertical wall are several Purple Tube Sponges and two lovely azure sponges along with lush coral growth. Here, also, it is possible that you will see a very large (2 m - 6 to 7 ft) Green Moray Eel, free swimming.
After swimming to the vertical wall along the reef slope, return to the mooring shallow as described above.

Occasionally at Carl's Hill there will be a strong current, and sometimes the current runs east toward the vertical wall.
If you are a cautious diver you may not wish to begin your dive by rushing down-current - but don't despair! Although there is no vertical wall west (to the left) of the mooring at Carl's Hill, the dive is still a very lovely one. Swim west at 15-21 m (50-70 ft), and you'll be surrounded by stony and soft corals and considerable sponge growths. You will pass an enormous green purple finger sponge, all entangled with itelf and curving away from the reef profile.
Shortly thereafter, at about 18 m (60 ft) you will see the largest Purple Tube Sponge we have yet discovered on Bonaire or Klein Bonaire; this sponge has in excess of 70 tubes!
Almost immediately beyond this giant tube sponge is a distinct buttress and sand valley, a good place to turn; come up to 7-12 m (23 to 40 ft), and return to the mooring. On your return you will see high-profile coral rocks along the drop-off and many cleaner stations.

Whichever way you choose to dive Carl's Hill, we know you will enjoy it.

*Fig. 123*
*Basket Starfish, curled up in a sea plume during the day and fully expanded at night.*

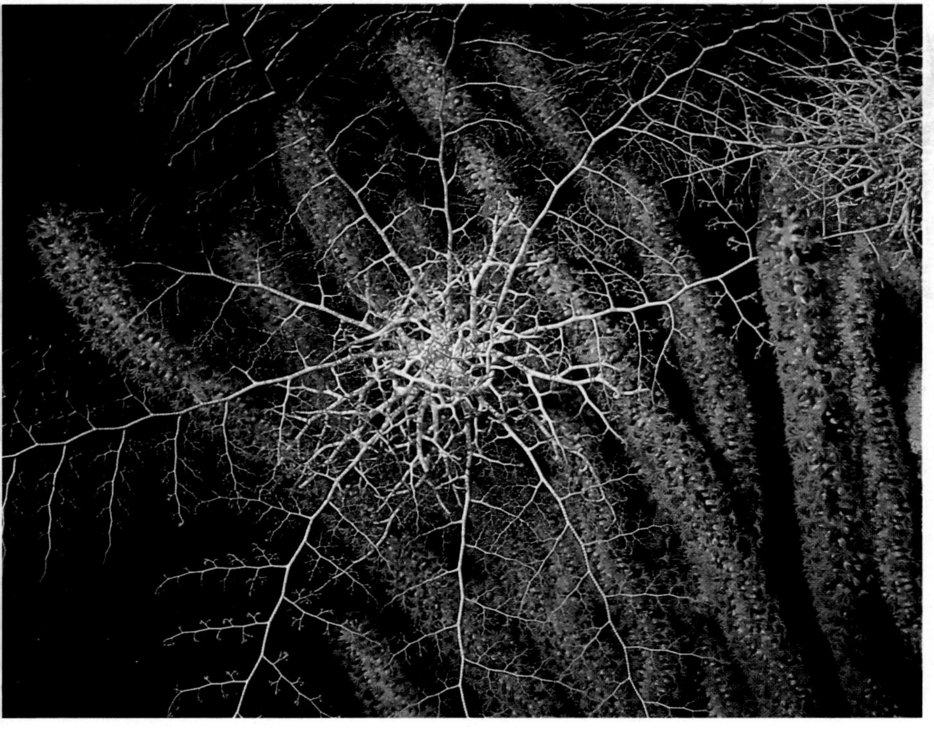

# Dive site:
# **Jerry's Jam** (Ebo's Special)

*Fig. 124*
*Shallow barrier with Orange Tube Coral.*

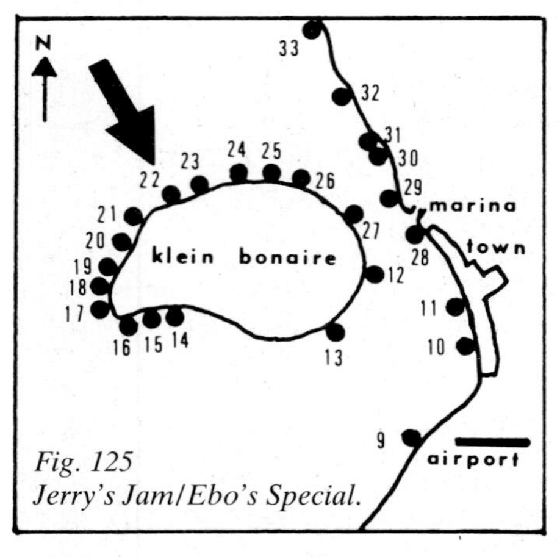


*Fig. 125*
*Jerry's Jam/Ebo's Special.*

1 *Boat dive*
2 *double barrel mooring / 5 m (17 ft)*
3 *n.a.*
4 *n.a.*
5 *all levels*
6 *no real drop-off*
7 *high*
8 *either way*
9 *27 m (90 ft)*
10 *very good snorkeling value.*

**Description**
The name of this dive site depends on the dive operation you have chosen. It was originally named after Bonaire's first dive guide, Hubert 'Ebo' Domacasse and later received its second name for photographe Jerry Greenberg and his cameras. According to the 1980 dive statistics it is one of the most popular dive sites. And for good reason.

The *shallow terrace* is extremely narrow and the reef begins to slope right down from the barrier of Elkhorn Coral, withou an actual drop-off. It is fascinating to look up from a depth of 27 m (90 ft) and to still be able to see the Elkhorn Coral at the surface.

On the *upper reef slope* are large Giant Brain Corals and towers of Mountainous Star Coral in all shapes, especially from 15 m (50 ft) up. The very high percentage of living coral is what makes the reef esthetically extremely attractive.
There are some buttresses but they are rather subtle.

The *lower reef slope* has the characteristi roof shingle formations of Sheet Corals and Mountainous Star Coral.

*Fig. 126*
*Looking up to the Elkhorn Coral at the surface.*

Gorgonians and black corals are not abundant.

There are no striking differences between the east and west side of the mooring. Going to the west (to the left facing the sea) you will notice that the percentage of living coral becomes progressively lower. After some 25 to 30 min. to the west you reach a wide reef slide, beginning with a near-vertical cut at 5 m (17 ft).

We can hardly speak of a *shallow terrace* in this area since it is so narrow that we have no real drop-off. Right below the surface and down to 2 or 3 m (7 or 10 ft) depth is a barrier of Elkhorn Coral, tightly cemented together in places by crustose coralline algae, and colonized by fire corals and lots of Orange Tube Coral. Next seaward the bottom is almost completely covered with Mountainous Star Coral, only interrupted by some patches of Yellow Pencil Coral. The usual Staghorn Coral is almost completely lacking in this area. Towards the east (to the right, facing the sea), at the edge of the elkhorn barrier at 3 m (10 ft), are two caves, close to one another, painted in orange, red, purple and pink by crustose coralline algae and Orange Tube Coral. A large Tiger Grouper is often seen hovering way in the back of one of the caves.

If you dive to the west and make it all the way to the slide, return shallow (above 6 m - 20 ft) and enjoy an extremely rich landscape. Just east of the slide begins a dense bed of Mountainous Star Coral (all heads of about the same size, as if some disturbance had occurred in the past and the whole area was recolonized by Mountainous Star Coral at the same time) with interspersed brain corals. The whole area is excellent for snorkeling.

*Fish life.* There are two outstanding characteristics of the fish life at Jerry's Jam/ Ebo's Special: the first is that there are always a *lot* of fish here; the second is the great *variety* of fish life. A person feeding fish here (not chumming up the yellowtails, but actually hand-feeding) is very likely to attract Spanish Hogfish, small groupers, Sergeant Majors, several species of parrotfish, and Yellowtail Snappers (of course). Some occasional handfeeders here include Scrawled Filefish, goatfish, grunts.

The crowd of feeders often attracts a Trumpetfish or two.

# Dive site:
# **Leonora's Reef**

*Fig. 127*
*Sandy Cober snorkels at Leonora's typical lush shallow water coral community.*

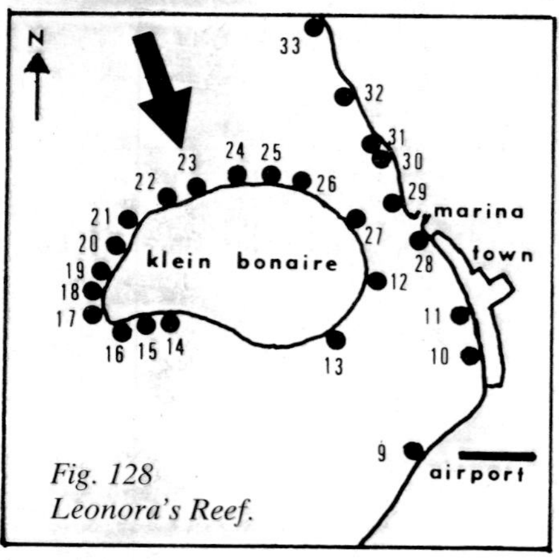


*Fig. 128*
*Leonora's Reef.*

1 *boat dive*
2 *double barrel mooring / 3 m (10 ft)*
3 *n.a.*
4 *n.a.*
5 *all levels*
6 *7-10 m (23-30 ft)*
7 *high (on the buttresses)*
8 *either way*
9 *21-24 m (70-80 ft)*
10 *good snorkeling value.*

*Fig. 129*
*Toppled head of Mountainous Star Coral, overgrown by algae.*

**Description**
Just below the *drop-off* Mountainous Star Coral and Giant Brain Coral are the most common coral species, along with Yellow Pencil Coral and Flower Coral. There are some very nice Pillar Coral formations just under the boat and slightly to the west of the mooring (left, facing the sea), unusual for this section of Klein Bonaire.

The *upper slope* is very nice, has a high percentage of live coral and a high relief. Flower Coral, Club Finger Coral and Yellow Pencil Coral are most abundant here. The slope is not rich in gorgonians, black corals, or sponges.
Buttresses occur on both sides of the mooring, but disappear towards the east (right, facing the sea).

Just west of the mooring, mortality is high on the *lower slope,* probably due to toppling of big coral heads, and algae have covered the dead coral blocks. Further west, but also east of the mooring, you will see a nice roof shingle community on the lower slope.

The *shallow terrace* is narrow, and generally covered extensively with Yellow Pencil Coral, fire corals and Mountainous Star Coral. Elkhorn Coral is found close to shore. The terrace is very much like the one at Knife which is relatively close (on a normal dive, swimming towards the east - right, facing the sea - you will easily reach the reef slide described under Knife-west).
*Fish life* includes some big groupers (Tiger Grouper, Yellowmouth Grouper). Even the less common Yellowfin Grouper can be observed in this area. 'Attack' Yellow-tail Snappers are in force here, too.

# Dive site:
# **Knife** (Korontin)

*Fig. 130*
*Elkhorn Coral.*

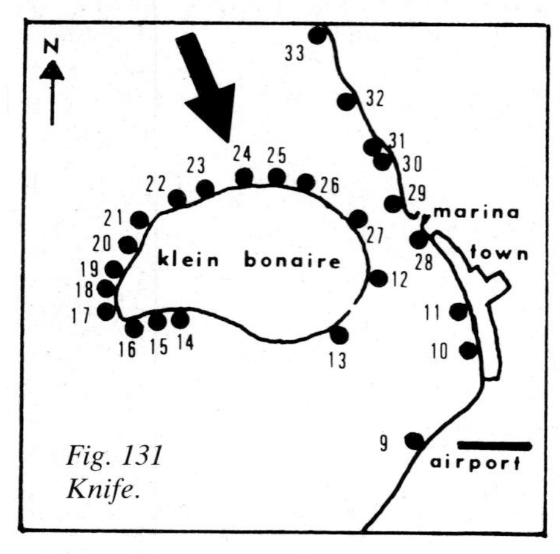


*Fig. 131*
*Knife.*

1. *boat dive*
2. *double barrel mooring / 4,5 m (15 ft)*
3. *n.a.*
4. *n.a.*
5. *all levels*
6. *6-10 m (20-30 ft)*
7. *high*
8. *east (right facing the sea)*
9. *24 m (80 ft)*
10. *excellent snorkeling value.*

**Description**
Knife is a typically lush Bonairean dive site, with nice coral formations. It is extremely good for snorkeling.

The *drop-off zone* is rather barren of coral growth. It is apparently an unstable environment. Gorgonians are more common here than on the slope and you will see the Encrusting Stinging Coral, Yellow Pencil Coral and the Encrusting Gorgonian.

On the *upper reef slope* are some fairly big towers of Mountainous Star Coral, otherwise the reef has not much relief and there is no distinct zonation. Neither gorgonians nor black corals are very abundant here. After a swim of about 25 min. to the east (right, facing the sea) you reach a barren channel, at least 30 m (100 ft) wide, that is apparently the result of a reef slide. This is a good turning point. Returning shallow is a must.
Going west (left, facing the sea) the reef is quite similar.
After some 25 min. you arrive at an other reef slide, less wide than the one to the east. From there you return shallow again.
The *shallow terrace* is extremely pretty with patches of Staghorn Coral and large clumps of the fragile Yellow Pencil Coral. Elkhorn Coral is present in less than 1 m (3 ft) of water. Straight up the terrace from the eastern reef slide you have a mixed community of Mountainous Star Coral, fire coral, Yellow Pencil Coral and Leaf Coral. You can swim inside a kind of mini-'lagoon', bordered with Elkhorn Coral, and separated from the shore by a massive , heavily encrusted elkhorn barrier. Inside the 'lagoon' are large heads of Mountainous Star Coral. West of the mooring the Staghorn Coral is more extensive, otherwise the coral community is quite similar to that towards the east.

*Fish life.* Of special interest on the reef slope are the French Angelfish. At Knife, at least 2 of these creatures are likely to approach a diver. They investigate each person curiously, looking for a handout, tasting exhaust bubbles and posing for

*Fig. 132*
*Knife is one of the loveliest spots for snorkeling.*

*Fig. 133*
*Mixed shallow-water coral community with fire coral, Mountainous Star Coral, Leaf Coral and Yellow Pencil Coral.*

photographs. When planning a dive here, add some cheese or a banana to your list of equipment; the French Angelfih will appreciate your thoughtfulness!
A relatively large number of Tiger Groupers seems to be characteristic for this area (both along the reef slope and shallow). This is a good site to watch the cleaning of groupers. One or two Ocean Triggerfish are often seen here. Near the mooring are some Bermuda Chubs which you can approach quite close. On the shallow terrace you wil find a lot more fish action than on the slope. The barren drop-off zone is a good place to look for well-camouflaged Peacock Flounders, Lizardfish and for the Yellowhead Jawfish that retreats into its burrow when a diver approaches.

# Dive site:
# **Sampler**

*Fig. 134*
*Ocean Triggerfish.*

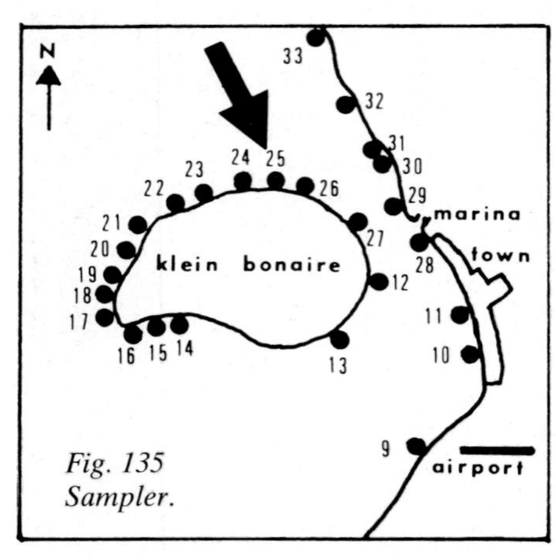


*Fig. 135*
*Sampler.*

1 *boat dive*
2 *double barrel mooring / 4 m (13 ft)*
3 *n.a.*
4 *n.a.*
5 *all levels*
6 *4-5 m (13-17 ft)*
7 *high*
8 *east (right facing the sea)*
9 *24 m (80 ft)*
10 *good snorkeling value.*

**Description**
Characteristic for this dive site are a narrow shallow terrace and a shallow *drop-off:* the reef begins to slope down from 4-5 m (13-17 ft). You will notice that there is a lot of sediment in the drop-off zone.

In the *upper reef slope* you find predominantly Mountainous Star Corals, including some very big heads. Some are partly dead and recolonized by Yellow Pencil Coral, Flower Coral or fire corals. The larger heads occur mainly east of the mooring where few sediment channels have developed. West (left, facing the sea) of the mooring coral cover in the upper slope is lower, there is more sediment and more sediment channels have developed. At about 18 m (60 ft), just west of the mooring a large coral head juts away from the reef slope. A careful observer may see as many as 3 groupers being cleaned at this cleaning station at once.
Generally speaking, the reef slope shows little zonation; few gorgonians and black corals occur (only some small colonies of black coral are found).

The *lower reef slope* has a higher algal cover, including crustose coralline algae, but you will also find some pretty roof shingle formations, made up of Sheet Corals and flattened Mountainous Star Coral.

The *shallow terrace* is a sandy plateau up to 3 m (10 ft), with scattered brain corals, Mustard Hill Coral and Mountainous Star Coral. From 3 m (10 ft) to the surface you find alternating patches of Yellow Pencil Coral, Elkhorn Coral and fire corals.
West of the mooring is a large patch of Staghorn Coral (a large school of Yellow Goatfish always seems to be around that area) and a beautiful colony of Pillar Coral.
*Fish life* includes some good-sized Yellowmouth Groupers, Tiger Groupers and of course the Yellowtail Snappers demonstrating that they are used to handfeeding. An Ocean Triggerfish is not uncommon here. Sampler also has a number of very

special residents: animals that are used to divers and to being fed. A diver is likely to meet 'Gladiator', a mature Spanish Hogfish. If a diver is feeding fish under the boat at Sampler, Gladiator is sure to be part of the crowd. He is the largest Spanish Hogfish in the area and his purplish color extends onto his body, in contrast to younger hogfish, whose purple and yellow areas are clearly distinct.
As the diver heads toward the drop-off, he is likely to be found by 'D'Artagnan', a French Angelfish who checks out every diver for possible handouts. D'Artagnan can be distinguished from other French Angelfish by the tiny white growth in the very center of his left eyeball.
Probably the most exciting characters here are the Spotted Moray Eels. 'Candide' is the most aggressive, frequently leaving the coral and heading toward a divers exhaust bubbles - nearsightedly hoping they are fish. Candide is just over 1 m (3 1/2 ft) long, very dark for a Spotted Moray, and 8 cm (3 inches) of his anal fin are missing just at his tail.
'Flattail' is smaller than Candide, just under 1 m (3 ft) long, and the tip of his tail isn't quite as pointed as on most Spotted Morays. Flattail is fairly gentle and will swim all around divers in the hope of finding someone with food.
Because of the many eels at Sampler it is suggested that divers do NOT bring fish down for feeding. Other foods are quite acceptable to Gladiator, D'Artagnan and the other fish; the eels will eat those foods but not be attracted by them.
Yellowhead Jawfish, those delicately colored yellow and blue creatures with the incongruous large black eyes, live in coarse sand/rubble areas and can be found at the top of the drop-off.

*Fig. 136*
*'D'Artagnan' the French Angelfish.*

# Dive site:
# **No Name** (Playita)

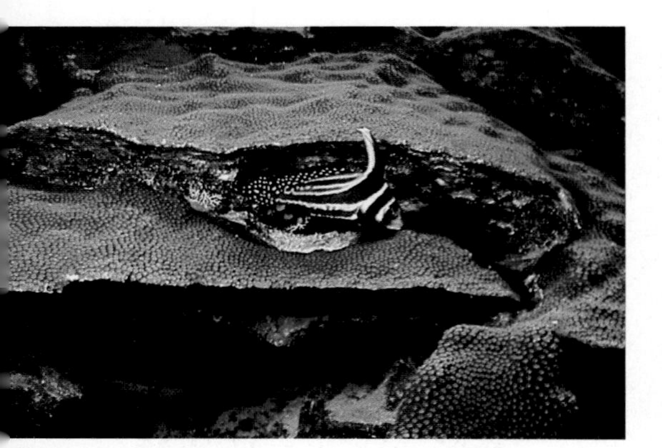

*Fig. 137*
*Spotted Drum.*

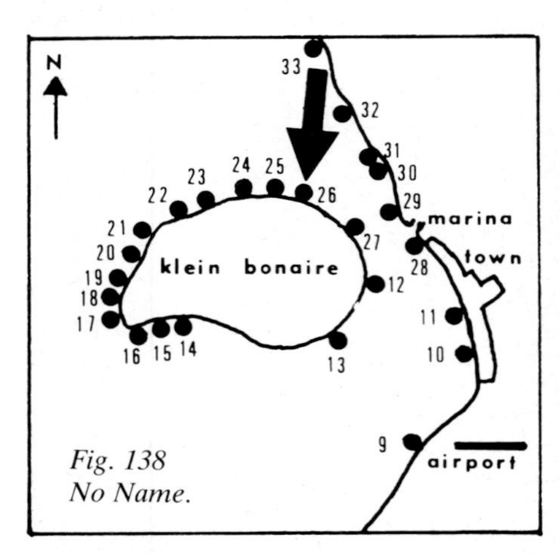


*Fig. 138*
*No Name.*

1 *boat dive (or shore dive for those who have themselves dropped off at the beach)*
2 *double barrel mooring / 3 m (10 ft)*
3 *easy*
4 *30 m (100 ft)*
5 *all levels*
6 *6 m (20 ft)*
7 *high*
8 *either way*
9 *24-27 m (80-90 ft)*
10 *good snorkeling value.*

**Description**
This site is situated along the only sizable, very popular beach at Klein Bonaire. The major hotels arrange picnics here and Bonaireans often spend a day or two here on weekends. It is also a good starting point for snorkeling trips.

The *drop-off* zone is shallow, sandy, rather barren, with some small brain corals and Mountainous Star Corals. Straight down from the mooring mortality among the corals is high (perhaps because of anchoring); Flower Coral and Yellow Pencil Coral are abundant.

On either side of the mooring the *reef slope* is very nice from 10 m (33 ft) down. From 24 m (80 ft) beautiful roof shingle formations are found. Black coral is fairly abundant, especially many young colonies are seen.

To the west (left, facing the sea) the reef

*Fig. 140*
*Sheet Coral (Agaricia lamarcki).*

*Fig. 139*
*Roof shingle community; to the left is Mountainous Star Coral, below center is one of the Sheet Corals (probably* Agaricia grahamae).

slope shows a system of buttresses and valleys. The reef has quite some relief and there are many hiding places. After about 35 min. to the west you reach a very protruding buttress, followed by a wide and deep valley. The buttress is covered with fire coral, Flower Coral and Yellow Pencil Coral. To the east (right, facing the sea) no buttresses are found.

*Shallow terrace.* Staghorn Coral is present from 3 m up. In the staghorn you will see Smallmouth- and French Grunts.
In the barren, sandy area above the drop-off are Yellow Goatfish, Lizardfish and Peacock Flounders. Bicolor Damselfish are found in the rubble along the edge of the staghorn fields. Close to the mooring the Staghorn Coral is absent and the bottom is nearly all sand.

*Fish life* includes good-sized Tiger Groupers, an occasional Yellowfin Grouper, Yellow mouth Groupers and big Schoolmasters. Spotted Moray Eels and squirrelfish occupy inconspicuous places in the coral. No Name is one of the few places on Klein Bonaire where divers can see Mullet. These browsing fish cruise the sand shallows and a diver or snorkeler can see a school of Mullet swimming in circles while foraging in the sand.

# Dive site:
# **Ebo's Reef**

*Fig. 141*
*Orange Sponge with Black-and-white Sea Lilies.*

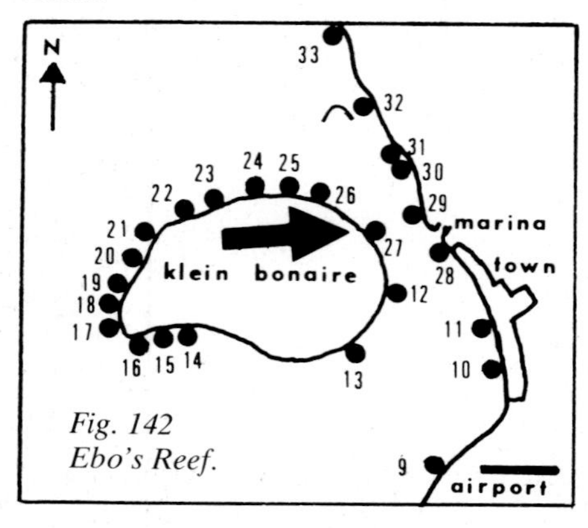


*Fig. 142*
*Ebo's Reef.*

1 *boat dive*
2 *engine blocs / 30 m (100 ft)*
3 *n.a.*
4 *n.a.*
5 *all levels*
6 *1-2 m (3-7 ft)*
7 *high on the buttresses*
8 *south (right, facing the sea)*
9 *27 m (90 ft)*
10 *limited snorkeling value.*

**Description**
This site has the highest density of black coral (at least for the species Dichotomous Black Coral) of all Bonaire. You will find black coral here as shallow as 6 m (20 ft) (please remember that black coral collecting is strictly prohibited on Bonaire). Also quite characteristic for this dive site are the many large orange sponges occurring here.

The *drop-off* in this area is very shallow. The sediments formed by bioerosion on the shallow terrace are discharged via wide sand/rubble valleys that alternate with pronounced buttresses.

The *reef slope* shows little zonation. The sand/rubble valleys are a very unstable habitat where numerous Do-not-touch-me Sponges occur. On the upper part of the buttresses the Yellow Pencil Coral occupies much space. Swimming north (left, facing the sea) the reef becomes more or less continuous after a while (the buttresses and valleys disappear). After 15-20 min.

*Fig. 143*
*Ebo's Reef has Bonaire's highest density of Dichotomous Black Coral.*

:o the north there is a wide reef slide with ots of coral rubble. Swimming toward the south you will find a series of buttresses, gradually becoming more pronounced because of the deeply cut alternating sand valleys. A short distance south of the mooring is a huge orange sponge with a dozen (or more) black and white crinoids on it. After 25-30 min. to the south are some beautiful Deepwater Gorgonians, characteristic for areas with fairly strong currents.

The *shallow terrace* is less than 2 m (7 ft) deep, sandy, with lots of small brain corals, Mustard Hill Coral, some Elkhorn Coral and Staghorn Coral. You'll see a variety of grazing fishes (mainly parrot-fish).

*Fish life.* Be prepared for the Yellowtail Snappers. You'll see quite a few Mahogany Snappers, some fairly big Tiger Groupers and an Ocean Triggerfish visits frequently. Near the buttress just north of the mooring you will find a school of goatfish which allow divers to approach within 1 m (3 ft) - quite close for these usually shy fish. One Spotted Scorpionfisch can almost always be found camouflaged along the buttress; occasionally two are seen. The buttress is also the home of a Coral Crab (usually nestled well under a ledge) and two Spotted Moray Eels.

*Fig. 144*
*Purple Tube Sponge with Black-and-white Sea Lilies.*

# Dive site:
# **Something Special** (Playa P'abou)

*Fig. 145*
*Garden Eels.*

**Description**
This site is well-known for its colony of Garden Eels that lives on the relatively shallow sand terrace (from 18 m - 60 ft - down). For safety reasons we do not recommend crossing the entrance of the marina to the north-west (right, facing the sea). However, as the area between Hotel Bonaire and the Marina is quite interesting it will be described as a separate dive under Front Porch (no. 29).

The *sand terrace* begins at 15 m (50 ft) just south of the entrance of the Marina and slopes down, both seaward and towards the south (left), to a depth of 30 m (100 ft) and beyond. Straight down from the mooring the sand terrace is at 24 m (80 ft). The Garden Eels will retreat into their burrows as you approach, but you can get as close as 2 m (7 ft) if you keep a low profile and breathe slowly.

Along the *reef slope* you'll find lots of

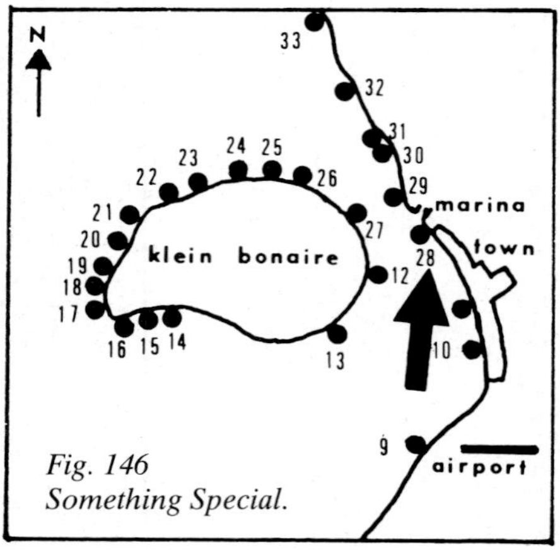

*Fig. 146*
*Something Special.*

1 *boat dive*
2 *double barrel mooring / 3 m (10 ft)*
3 *n.a.*
4 *n.a.*
5 *all levels*
6 *7-9 m (23-30 ft)*
7 *moderate*
8 *south-east (left, facing the sea)*
9 *27 m (90 ft)*
10 *limited snorkeling value.*

*Fig. 147*
*Aerial photograph showing the course of the deep sand terrace (eel garden).*

sponges, especially the Purple Bleeding Sponge, living in symbiosis with an orange colonial anemone. Unfortunately there is also a lot of trash on the reef. You may see a 1.80 m (6 ft) Tarpon hanging motionless just off the reef slope and there are abundant Creole Fish (frequently having large parasites just below the eyes), Smallmouth Grunts and Mahogany Snappers. In the shallow sandy area in between the mooring and the Marina are lots of Scorpionfish and Spotted Moray Eels. At the tip of the southern groin at the Marina entrance you will see abundant Schoolmasters, Bluestriped Grunts, Sergeant Majors, Bermuda Chubs and Black Margates.

*Fig. 148*
*Purple Bleeding Sponge.*

*Fig. 149*
*Tarpon.*

# Dive site:
# **Front Porch**

*Fig. 150*
*Ocellated Frogfish.*

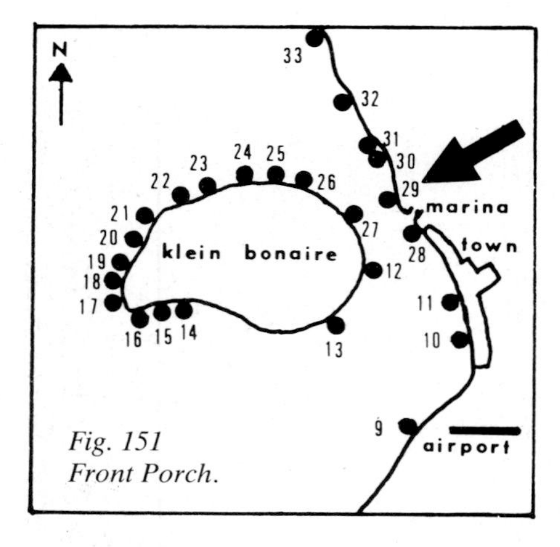


*Fig. 151*
*Front Porch.*

1 *shore dive*
2 —
3 *very easy*
4 *25 m (80 ft)*
5 *all levels*
6 *6-9 m (20-30 ft)*
7 *low, increasing to the north (right, facing the sea)*
8 *two completely different dives in either direction*
9 *21-24 m (70-80 ft)*
10 *limited snorkeling value.*

**Description**
This is where you will make your warm-up dive when you stay at Hotel Bonaire and/ or dive with Bonaire Scuba Center. Unfortunately coral mortality is high in front of the Hotel, but this is made up by prolific sponges and tame fish.
Reef development is better to the north (right, facing the sea), and an entirely different, but interesting dive can be made going south towards the marina.

You enter from the Bonaire Scuba Center pier. There is a narrow sand flat that begins to slope down already at 3 m (10 ft). The pier itself is quite interesting: lots of Orange Tube Coral, the delicately branched coral *Stylaster* hidden in small crevices, Redlip Blennies and schooling juvenile French Grunts. Just off the pier there are often some large Barracudas, abundant Sergeant Majors and right away you will be surrounded by Yellowtail Snappers.

On the *reef slope* are many Purple Tube Sponges and sprawling purple sponges. Among the living coral the Cavernous Star Coral dominates. Swimming to the north (right, facing the sea) you will notice that mortality is highst near the mooring site of the 'Gypsy Girl'. In this area, at 7 m (23 ft), you can see an old anchor, overgrown by all kinds of invertebrates.

*Fish life.* Along the reef slope Graysbys and Rock Hinds are common. There are schools of goatfish, Creole Fish, Sergeant Majors and plenty of Yellowtail Snappers.

If you choose to dive *towards the marina,* don't expect to find a beautiful reef there. But, if nothing else, there is less garbage in this direction. The *reef slope* is very gentle and consists of alternating ridges of coarse rubble and rivers of fine rubble and sand. There is no living coral here. First you will pass an extensive field of Do-not-touch-me Sponges.
This is by far the most common sponge in this area. Look inside the large opening for a small goby: it is swimming frantically against the current created by the sponge that tirelessly pumps water through its

system to filter food particles.
Further on purple sprawling sponges and many Pink-tipped Anemones are added. Associated with these anemones are Pederson's Cleaning Shrimp, Spotted Cleaning Shrimp and Little Brown Spotted Shrimp. Characteristic for the rubble habitat are the Bicolor Damselfish and the Pygmy Angelfish. There is no other place on Bonaire where Pygmy Angelfish are so abundant. Look also for Spotted- and Goldentail Moray Eels in the rubble. Scorpionfish are common here; they blend in perfectly with the rocks. And watch the Yellowhead Jawfish, curiously protruding from their holes and backing into them when you come close. The observant diver may even see the juvenile Queen Triggerfish that looks like a miniature replica of the adult, and tiny, slowly moving, black 'balls' of about 1/2 cm (1/5 inch): juvenile trunkfish.
There is no need to go much beyond a depth of 20 m (60-70 ft) and, although it is a fairly long swim, it is worth it to go all the way to the last ridge of rubble at about the center of the Marina bungalow complex. In shallow water you can find Snook here.

*Fig. 152*
*Aerial view of Front Porch and Hotel Bonaire.*

*Fig. 153*
Stylaster *is found in the crevices of the pier at Front Porch.*

*Fig. 154*
*Do-not-touch-me Sponge.*

*Fig. 155*
*Snook.*

# Dive site:
# **La Machaca**

*Fig. 156*
*Wreck at La Machaca.*

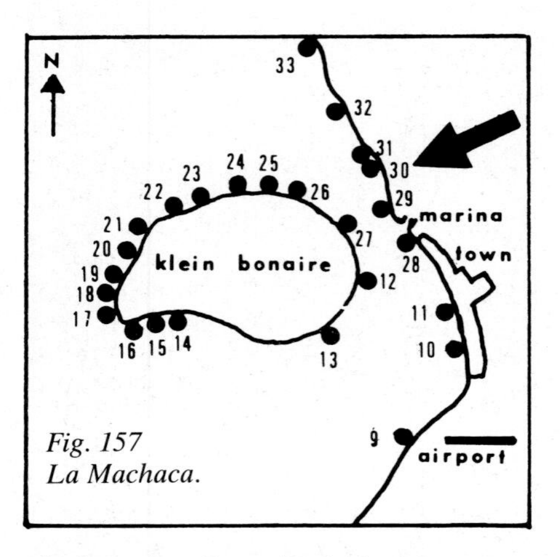


*Fig. 157*
*La Machaca.*

*1 shore dive (from the dock of Captain Don's Habitat)*
*2 none*
*3 easy*
*4 45 m (150 ft)*
*5 all levels*
*6 6-10 m (20-33 ft)*
*7 fairly high*
*8 north-west (right, facing the sea)*
*9 36 m (120 ft)*
*10 very good snorkeling value.*

**Description**
This is an easy, relaxed dive. Divers staying at Captain Don's Habitat will make their warm-up dive here. You will see just about everything that you can expect on the Bonairean reefs.
Even some black coral, but you need to have both eyes wide open. Entering from the main dock you just follow the rope with the clorox bottles. At a depth of 6 m (20 ft) the shallow terrace begins to slope down. At 10 m (33 ft) you reach a small *wreck* sunk there by Captain Don. The wreck is not much colonized yet, but fire coral and Black Wire Corals have begun to grow on the hull. Sergeant Majors have their nests on the hull; the nests are visible as large dark purple patches and represent the eggs on tiny stalks, but are best spotted by the frantic defensive behavior of the male parent fish guarding the eggs. The wreck is the home of an old Tiger Grouper ('old' Tiger Groupers are recognized by the fringes on their fins) and two large Black Margates, just under the bow, while a spotted Moray Eel is found nearby. The Tiger Grouper can change coloration so quickly that you might think there are two of them. It may enter one porthole in a dark pattern and swim out another in pale grey colour. The cleaning of the Tiger Grouper is fascinating. A typical cleaning scene will show the grouper with its mouth wide open, two gobies working its mouth, one goby on the head and a juvenile Spanish Hogfish covering the body.
Take your time, and your camera.

The *reef slope* begins at 10 m (33 ft). The lower edge of the reef is at 36 m (120 ft), where you can have a quick look at the Garden Eels in the sand terrace. On your way down you may have an encounter with a 1.50 m (5 ft) Tarpon. Turn north-west (right, facing the sea) and start your ascent. On the *lower slope* are beautiful roof shingle formations of Sheet and Scroll Coral. Coming up the slope you will see some fairly big heads of Giant Brain Coral and of course the Mountainous Star Coral. Gorgonians are more common on the

*Fig. 158*
*Aerial view of La Machaca, Cliff and Captain Don's Habitat.*

*Fig. 159*
*Tiger Grouper under the wreck at La Machaca.*

*upper reef slope.* Near the turning point (marked with a float at 10 m; 33 ft) is a nice colony of Pillar Coral.

Return over the *shallow terrace.* A field of Staghorn Coral extends from 6 m (20 ft) to 3 m (10 ft). More shallow the fire coral becomes abundant and you can find some Fused Staghorn Coral, a finely branched relative of the common Staghorn Coral. Also characteristic for the shallow area are the small colonies of Mustard Hill Coral. Lush Elkhorn Coral reaches nearly up to the surface. Schools of surgeonfish, along with parrotfish, Yellow Goatfish, Trumpetfish or a Spanish Hogfish rove through the Staghorn and Elkhorn Coral in search of food.

*Fig. 160*
*Fused Staghorn Coral.*

# Dive site:
# **Cliff**

*Fig. 161*
*Vertical wall at Cliff.*

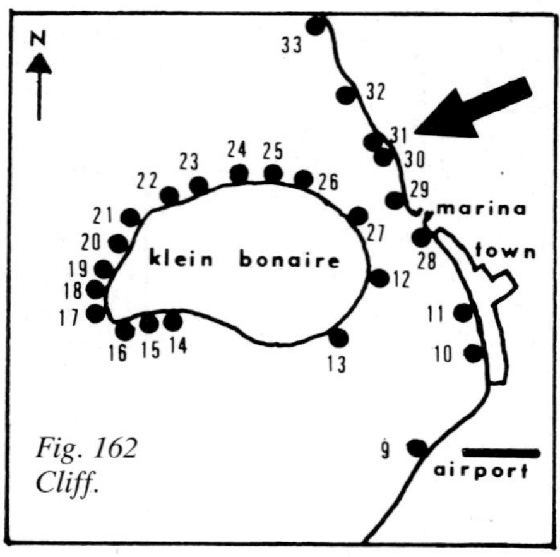


*Fig. 162*
*Cliff.*

1 *boat dive or shore dive*
2 *double barrel mooring / 2,5 m (8 ft)*
3 *easy*
4 *35 m (120 ft)*
5 *all levels*
6 *9 m (30 ft)*
7 *upper reef slope: high; lower slope: moderate*
8 *straight down from the mooring*
9 *18 m (60 ft)*
10 *very good snorkeling value.*

**Description**
To get there by car you drive north from town to Captain Don's Habitat. Take the unpaved road to the left immediately past the Habitat and drive to the edge of the cliff. You enter from the small beach through a channel in the elkhorn-fire cora barrier. The channel itself is carpeted wit Club Finger Coral.
Watch out for the sea urchins as you pass through the channel.
Seaward of the barrier the *shallow terrace* is a barren sand flat with coral rubble, some fire coral, Mustard Hill Coral and brain corals.

The *upper reef slope* is a vertical wall, from 9 m (30 ft) down to 18 m (60 ft). Th wall is covered with flattened Cavernous Star Coral, Sheet Corals, Encrusting Gorgonians with their long swaying polyps encrusting sponges, Black Wire Corals and other small black corals. Plenty of subjects here for the macrophotographer.

Along the upper edge of the slope, you will observe a slow, but almost continuous drizzle of sediments going down. This makes you realize that reef-building is a dynamic process.

*Fig. 163*
*Incredible healing.*

Of the 100 tons of calciumcarbonate produced per hectare by the corals annually (40 tons per acre), some 25 tons per hectare (10 tons per acre) are consumed by grazers such as the Long-spined Sea Urchin and Fishes and excreted again after these animals have digested the algae that grow on the limestone. These 25 tons of fine calciumcarbonate sand produced by the herbivore grazers gradually flow down the reef slope.

*Fish life.* The shallow sand terrace is a typical habitat for Lizardfish, Peacock Flounder, Scorpionfish and an occasional Yellowhead Jawfish. At the wall you will see plenty of Royal Grammas and Yellowtail Snappers, along with other common reef inhabitants. To the south (left, facing the sea), is a favourite feeding spot for divers.

At 21-27 m (70-90 ft), especially on the left of the mooring (facing the sea) one or two Tarpon are frequently seen. These fish are well over 1 m (4-5 ft) long, with huge silvery scales.

They don't appear frightened of divers, but they do keep their distance.

Sometimes a Stoplight Parrotfish is seen at Cliff with a deep scar, apparently from a serious wound, in the dorsal portion of tis body.

The whole area in between Cliff and Captain Don's Habitat is excellent for snorkeling.

# Dive site:
# **Small Wall**

*Fig. 164*
*Orange sponge and Black Wire Corals at Small Wall.*

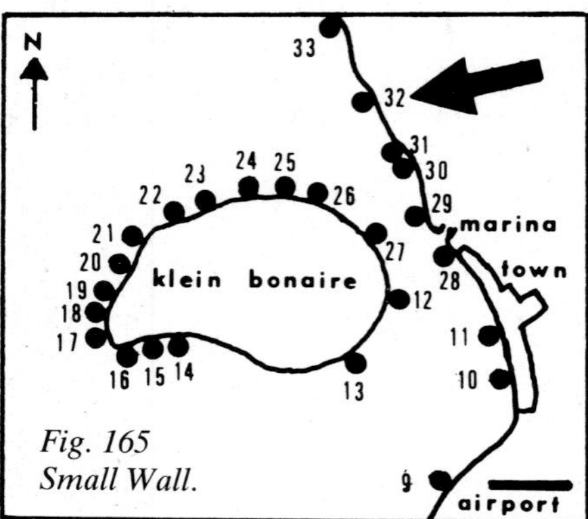


*Fig. 165*
*Small Wall.*

1 *boat dive (shore dive for those staying at the Cocohut Beach)*
2 *double barrel mooring / 4 m (13 ft)*
3 *easy*
4 *70 m (230 ft)*
5 *all levels*
6 *7-10 m (23-33 ft)*
7 *high*
8 *south-east (left, facing the sea)*
9 *27 m (90 ft)*
10 *limited snorkeling value.*

**Description**
This dive site is situated off the 'Cocohut Beach' and is therefore a shore dive only for those who are staying there or have made special arrangements with the owner. As the name suggests this site is characterized by the presence of a (small) *wall* (fig. 166). You will find the wall just southeast (left, facing the sea) of the mooring. It starts at 12 m (40 ft) and goes down to about 20 m (67 ft). Gorgonians are abundant at the upper edge of the wall, and along the vertical slope are sponges, Black Wire Coral, large flattened Sheet Corals, Fungus Coral and abundant Cavernous Star Coral. The Encrusting Gorgonian has occupied a considerable surface area on the wall.
At the lower edge you will see a small cave. Royal Gramma are plentiful along the wall. From the entrance of the cave you will see several sets of white whiskers belonging to Banded Coral Shrimp.

Along the *reef slope* are some nice roof shingle formations of Mountainous Star Coral and Sheet and Scroll Corals from 27 m (90 ft) down.

On the *shallow terrace* the Staghorn Coral extends from 3 m (10 ft) down to the beginning of the drop-off. In between are patches of Yellow Pencil Coral, some brain corals and small heads of Mountainous Star Coral. Just off the shore is a narrow, heavily encrusted barrier of Elkhorn Coral with fire corals and Encrusting Colonial Anemones.

*Fish life.* Along the reef slope a pair of Scrawled Filefish is frequently seen. Furthermore you may see some Barracuda, snappers, Tiger Grouper and Tarpon. The rubble-sand area of the drop-off zone is a good place to look for Lizardfish and Peacock Flounder. Trumpetfish are plentiful on the shallow terrace.

*Fig. 166*
*View of the shallow terrace, the vertical wall and the reef slope at Small Wall.*

*Fig. 167*
*Tarpons.*

# Dive site:
# **Petries Pillar**

*Fig. 168*
*Shallow terrace with Brown Chromis and Yellow Goatfish.*

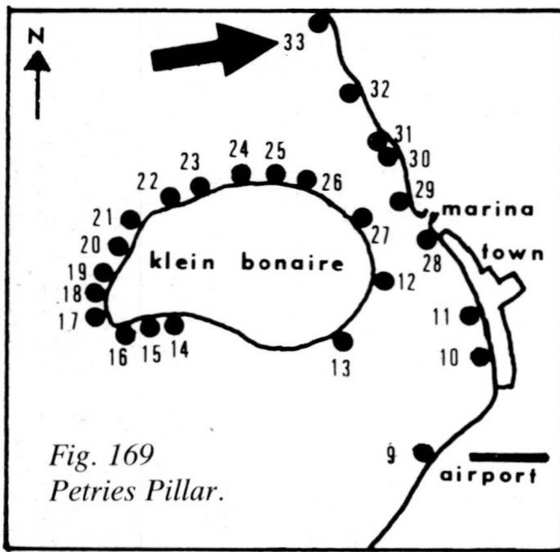


*Fig. 169*
*Petries Pillar.*

1 *boat or shore dive*
2 *double barrel mooring / 10 m (33 ft)*
3 *fairly easy*
4 *90 m (300 ft)*
5 *all levels*
6 *10-12 m (33-40 ft)*
7 *fairly high*
8 *either way*
9 *27 m (90 ft)*
10 *fair snorkeling value.*

**Description**
This site was named for a colony of Pillar Coral that towers some 1.20 m (4 ft) above the reef face, just north-west (right, facing the sea) of the mooring. If you want to dive from the shore, take the scenic road from town towards Gotomeer. At 700 m (2.300 ft) after the last house of the residential area past the waterplant you take the unpaved road to the left that heads down to the sea. You enter through an opening in the Elkhorn Coral, north-west (right) of the mooring, just left of the shortest of two dam-like structures consisting of dead coral blocks.

The *drop-off zone* is rather barren and the *reef slope* seems to have suffered from sediments. Gorgonians are present on the upper reef slope, but black corals are not very abundant. The lower reef slope is attractive with its formations of Sheet and Scroll Corals.

*Fig. 170*
*Pillar Coral.*

On the *shallow terrace* a fairly extensive zone of Staghorn Coral starts between 8 and 6 m (27 and 20 ft). Yellow Pencil Coral is found along the deeper limit of the staghorn zone and in patches in between the Staghorn Coral. Interspersed with the Staghorn Coral are the Pink-tipped Anemone, small heads of Mountainous Star Coral, brain corals and fire coral. The Elkhorn Coral starts at a depth of about 3 m (10 ft) and forms a barrier, tightly knit together by crustose coralline algae and covered in places with Encrusting Colonial Anemones.

*Fish life.* There are usually some Barracuda in this area, and you will see Tiger Groupers and Yellowmouth Groupers.

*Fig. 171*
*Shallow water elkhorn barrier with Leafy Stinging Coral.*

# Dive site:
# **Oil Slick Leap**

*Fig. 172*
*Cliff wall with Elkhorn Coral.*

**Description**
This site is situated opposite the Hilltop Hotel and was named at the time that the area was considered as a possible location for building the oil terminal. It has not been dived frequently.

The *drop-off zone* (8-12 m; 27-40 ft) has a luxuriant gorgonian fauna, but rather few living corals.
Little zonation along the *reef slope,* but from 30 m (100 ft) down typical roof shingle structures of Mountainous Star Coral, Sheet and Scroll corals are found. The shingles are favourite hiding places for the Banded Coral Shrimp. Gorgonians are abundant again on the lower reef slope. Black coral is not common in this area.

The *shallow terrace* is quite narrow at the mooring site.
From 8 m (27 ft) upward you first have a narrow zone with Staghorn Coral. From 6-

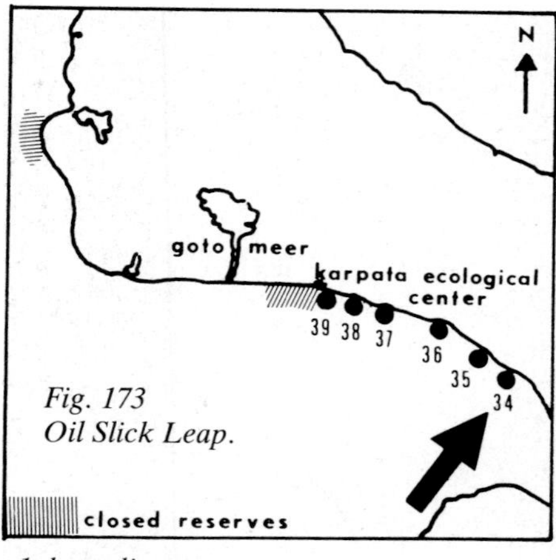


*Fig. 173*
*Oil Slick Leap.*

1 *boat dive*
2 *double barrel mooring / 9 m (30 ft)*
3 *n.a.*
4 *n.a.*
5 *all levels*
6 *10 m (33 ft)*
7 *high*
8 *either way*
9 *30 m (100 ft)*
10 *limited snorkeling value.*

*Fig. 174*
*Spiny Lobster.*

3 m (20-10 ft) you will find a lot of Yellow Pencil Coral, fire corals, different species of brain coral and gorgonians. The upper 3 m (10 ft) is a near vertical cliff. As this coast is rather exposed many of the fragile corals are broken by wave action and you will find a barren zone with coral rubble at the base of the cliff. This rubble zone is the home of many Bicolor Damselfish. The cliff itself is covered with pink and purple crustose coralline algae, the Orange Tube Coral, Leaf Coral, fire coral and gorgonians. It is an interesting and very colorful zone.
Just west of the mooring (right, facing the sea) is a nice formation of Pillar Coral at 4 m (13 ft). Further to the west (after about 10 min.) the terrace widens somewhat and a zone with elkhorn Coral appears. Between 3 and 6 m (10 and 20 ft) the terrace is rather barren. East of the mooring (left, facing the sea) at first the terrace is quite narrow and has a lush gorgonian growth. Among the branches of the gorgonians is a good place to look for well-camouflaged small filefish. After some 5 min. to the east the terrace widens and Staghorn Coral becomes more abundant. At 10 min. east Elkhorn Coral appears along with Plate Fire Coral.

*Fish life.* It becomes clear from the behaviour of the Yellowtail Snappers that they are not much used (yet) to being fed. Although the fish fauna is not spectacular you may expect Barracuda, Tiger Grouper and Yellowmouth Grouper. You will also see French and Queen Angelfish and Scrawled or Whitespotted Filefish.

*Fig. 175*
*White-spotted Filefish.*

# Dive site:
# **1000 Steps** (Piedra Haltu)

*Fig. 176*
*Purple Tube Sponge.*

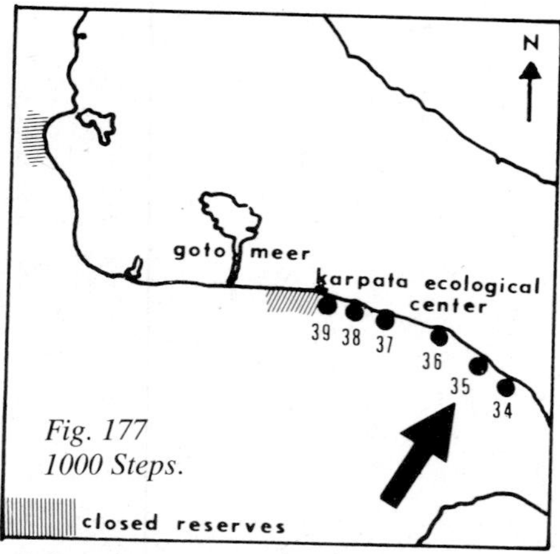


*Fig. 177*
*1000 Steps.*

1 *boat dive or shore dive*
2 *double barrel mooring / 6 m (20 ft)*
3 *easy*
4 *60 m (200 ft)*
5 *all levels*
6 *10 m (33 ft)*
7 *high*
8 *either way*
9 *27 m (90 ft)*
10 *limited snorkeling value.*

**Description**

Usually visited by boat, but also a convenient shore dive for those who don't mind the steps. Drive north from town along the scenic road towards Gotomeer until you reach the entrance of the 'Radio Nederland Wereld Omroep' transmitting station. This is where you park and walk down the steps to a large rubble beach. The best place to enter is somewhat right of where the steps come down to the beach.

Near the mooring, just above the *drop-off,* a big tower of Mountainous Star Coral functions as a cleaning station serviced by juvenile Spanish Hogfish and Bluehead Wrasses.

*Fig. 178*
*Many excavated Mountainous Star Corals serve as cleaning stations.*

There are several more of these big towers in the drop-off zone and they are nearly all cleaning stations. Gorgonians are abundant in this zone. The *upper reef slope* is dominated by Mountainous Star Coral, some of which form roof shingle structures. The *lower reef slope* has abundant Sheet and Scroll Coral.

*South-east* (left, facing the sea) of the mooring sponges and gorgonians become more abundant. To the *north-west* (right) the Sheet and Scroll Coral on the lower slope have suffered from sedimentation. Again gorgonians become more and more prolific in the drop-off zone.

The *shallow terrace* is sandy with gorgonians, scattered Elkhorn Coral and head corals. Most of the Staghorn Coral is broken.

*Fish life.* This is a good place to watch the cleaning symbiosis. Fish feeding attracts a fairly wide variety of fish here: parrotfish, Sergeant Majors, wrasses, small groupers, etc. An alert diver checking the hollowed-out bases of coral heads is likely to find the uncommon Shovelnosed Lobster.

# Dive site:
# **Ol' Blue**

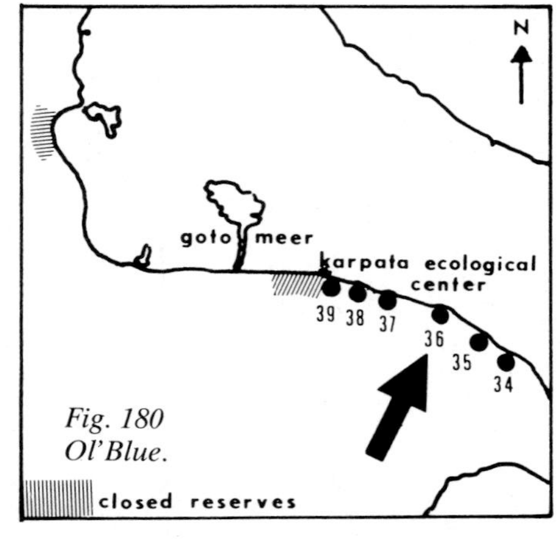


*Fig. 180*
*Ol'Blue.*

*Fig. 179*
*Lisa Bateman examines a finger sponge at Ol'Blue.*

1 *shore dive*
2 *planned*
3 *easy*
4 *30 m (100 ft)*
5 *all levels*
6 *9 m (30 ft)*
7 *high*
8 *either way*
9 *27 m (90 ft)*
10 *limited snorkeling value.*

**Description**

Drive north from town along the scenic road to Gotomeer and past the transmittin station of Radio Nederland Wereld Omroep. You will see Ol'Blue as the white coral rubble beach at the point where the road descends to the ocean and the cliff bends away from the road.

Swim out over the *shallow terrace* towards the drop-off. At first the bottom is predominantly sand and rubble, then some Mountainous Star Coral and gorgonians appear, gradually changing into a mixed Mountainous Star Coral-gorgonian community close to the drop-off. Just below the drop-off Yellow Pencil Coral is abundant and on the *upper reef slope* you find mostly Mountainous Star Coral, with some Flower Coral. Typical Sheet and Scroll Coral are present on the *lower reef slope*, but they have suffered from sediments. Going *west* (right, facing the sea)

Fig. 181
*Horse-eye Jacks.*

you will notice that after some 20 to 25 min. the number of gorgonians along the slope increases and the reef shows more variation. Return over the drop-off zone where gorgonians are prolific.
To the *east* (left, facing the sea) the influence of sedimentation on the deep reef is more pronounced and gorgonians are more abundant. After 20 to 30 min. to the east (that is well outside the bay), close to the cliff at a depth of 6 m (20 ft), you find three large and two smaller limestone blocks, apparently broken off the cliff. They are densely covered with gorgonians, sponges and, amongst others, Cavernous Star Coral. They offer shelter to a variety of fish. One of the blocks has a Pillar Coral on top. They are quite attractive, also for snorkeling, if you don't mind snorkeling for 20 to 30 min. and back.

*Fish life.* There are some Barracuda, Black Durgons, small Tiger- and Yellowmouth Groupers. Yellowtail Snappers, Schoolmasters and Mahogany Snappers are abundant. You may see the Scrawled Filefish and perhaps a school of curious Horse-eye Jacks.

# Dive site:
# **Rappel**

*Fig. 182*
*Colorful notch in the cliff just below the surface: crustose coralline algae, Orange Tube Coral and encrusting sponges.*

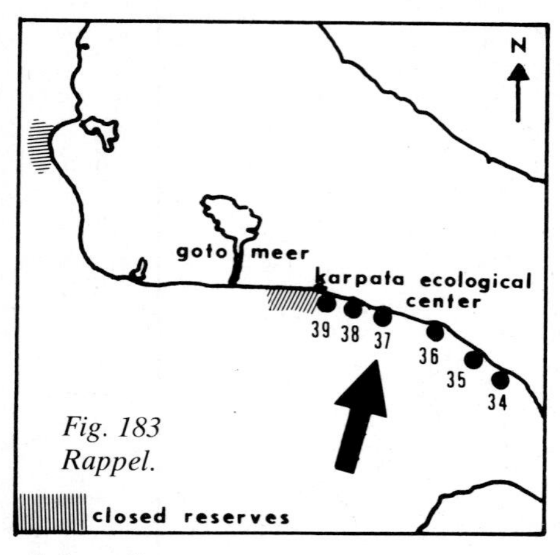


*Fig. 183*
*Rappel.*

1 *boat dive*
2 *double barrel mooring / 11 m (37 ft)*
3 *n.a.*
4 *n.a.*
5 *all levels*
6 *11-12 m (37-40 ft)*
7 *very high*
8 *either way*
9 *30 m (100 ft)*
10 *good snorkeling value when sea is calm.*

**Description**
This is one of the more spectacular dives. The terrace is extremely narrow and the boat has to be moored very close to the shore which is a sheer cliff. This cliff continues underwater almost vertically down to a depth of 9 m (30 ft).
The mooring is placed on a coral promontory, close to the drop-off.

Along the *upper reef slope* are a few vertical coral promontories, the deepest going down to 80 ft with a ledge. The ceiling of this ledge is the home of many Royal Grammas that swim in a décor of purple coralline algae and encrusting sponges. The more shallow promontory is abundantly covered with star corals, especially Cavernous Star Coral. A notch is visible at 16 m (53 ft).
The upper slope has massive boulders of Mountainous Star Coral and large Giant Brain Corals. To the west (right, facing the sea) at 18 m (60 ft) is a huge, toppled, Giant Brain Coral, still partly alive but excavated by sea urchins. There are few gorgonians and black corals, not many sponges, but yet the reef slope offers a beautiful scenery because there is hardly any mortality.

The *lower reef slope* is densely covered with Sheet and Scroll Corals, growing as roof shingles. This roof shingle community continues well below 50 m (170 ft). The reef slopes on both sides of the mooring are quite similar.

The *shallow terrace* is covered with massive Mountainous Star Corals. Giant Brain Coral and Yellow Pencil Coral are also common and occasional patches of Staghorn Coral are found.
The exposed cliff wall, from 9 m (30 ft) up to the surface is covered with corals and gorgonians. In the upper 3 m (10 ft) Orange Tube Coral is abundant. The notch in the cliff just below the surface is unbelievably colorful with its coralline algae and encrusting sponges. On a calm day you will have the opportunity to explore this colorful world.
Towards the east (left, facing the sea) the

*Fig. 184*
*Coral promontory just below the drop-off.*

*Fig. 185*
*Toppled Giant Brain Coral, eroded at the base.*

*Fig. 186*
*Cliff wall with stony and soft corals.*

structure and species composition of the shallow terrace changes dramatically: about 100 m (330 ft) from the mooring the terrace goes up from 9 m (30 ft) to about 5 m (17 ft) and a field of heavily encrusted Staghorn Coral rubble begins. Towards the shore is a narrow zone of Elkhorn Coral and near the drop-off Club Finger Coral and patches of Yellow Pencil Coral are abundant.

*Fish life.* The lush coral growth at Rappel provides homes for an unusual variety of fish - if the diver is sharp-eyed enough to find them. Green Moray Eels are found frequently along the cliff and the shallow terrace. An occasional Spiny Lobster, school of bait fish, Squid or Marbled Grouper highlights a dive.

At the time of this writing, a 15 cm (6 inches) orange Seahorse lives in the coral near the mooring at Rappel. Dive guides can find it for you, and will carefully replace it in its niche.

Other reef life includes several Tiger Groupers, Yellowmouth Groupers and you may see a 1 m (4 ft) Yellowfin Grouper. Horse-eye Jacks can also be expected. Above the mazes of the coral reef, Yellowtail Snappers in groups, not mobs, greet divers and are looking for a handout (chumming with bread will turn the group into a mob). The Rappel welcoming committee is unique, though, because along with the Yellowtails is Sir Timothy, a Spotted Trunkfish. Ever since the mooring was placed (June, 1981) Sir Timothy has been greeting divers curiously, and gently taking some banana or cheese right from their hands.

You don't need to look for Timothy - he'll find you.

# Dive site:
# La Dania's Leap

*Fig. 187*
*Vertical reef slope with sponges, Black Wire Corals and small Dichotomous Black Coral (lower right corner). Diver: Christie Dovale.*

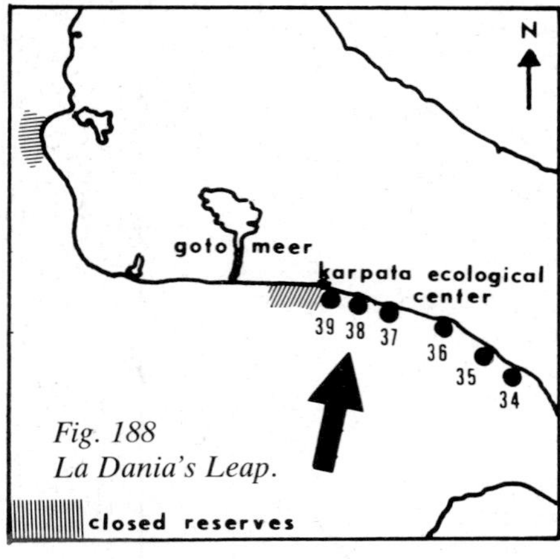


*Fig. 188*
*La Dania's Leap.*

1 *boat dive*
2 *double barrel mooring / 6 m (20 ft)*
3 *n.a.*
4 *n.a.*
5 *all levels*
6 *9 m (30 ft)*
7 *high*
8 *either way, but wall is deeper towards the west (Karpata)*
9 *30-33 m (100-110 ft)*
10 *limited snorkeling value.*

**Description**
This is one of the more sensational dive sites of Bonaire, not so much as fish life is concerned, but in terms of reef structure. There are vertical walls on both sides of the mooring and to fully enjoy this site you should by prepared for a rather deep dive. So don't plan La Dania's as the second dive of a day.

The *reef slope* becomes gradually steeper from 9 m (30 ft) down, until it gets vertical at about 25 m (83 ft) down to a depth of 33 to 36 m (110-120 ft).
To the *east* (left, facing the sea) the steep slope consists of a series of buttresses and deeply cut valleys. At the lower edge of the vertical wall the slope continues at an angle of about 30° as a sand terrace. Gently sloping buttresses have developed on the sand, in line with the more shallow steep buttresses (fig. 189).

On the vertical wall you find large flattened Sheet Corals, Black Wire Corals, and abundant but small black corals (as many as 10 per sq. m - 1 per sq. ft). The deep buttresses are covered with flattened Sheet and Scroll Corals. After some 20 min. to the east the deep vertical wall changes into a series of buttresses that run from 15 m (50 ft) down to about 40 m (130 ft).
They support a shallow vertical wall that runs from 10 m (33 ft) down to 15 m (50 ft) (fig. 190). This wall is covered with Cavernous Star Coral, Encrusting Gorgonian, sponges and abundant gorgonians along its upper edge.
The end of the deep vertical wall seems a

*Fig. 189*
*Reef profile just east (left) of the mooring: steep buttresses from 9-25 m, followed by a vertical slope down to 33 m and gently sloping buttresses on the deep terrace.*

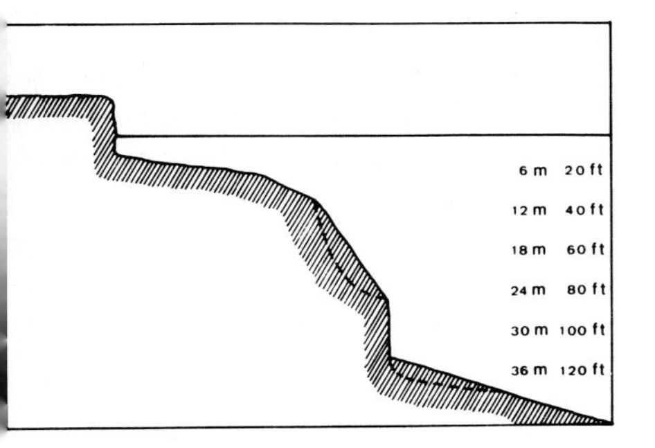


*Fig. 190*
*Change in the reef profile further east (left) of the mooring: short vertical slope from 10-15 m, followed by steep butresses down to 36 m.*

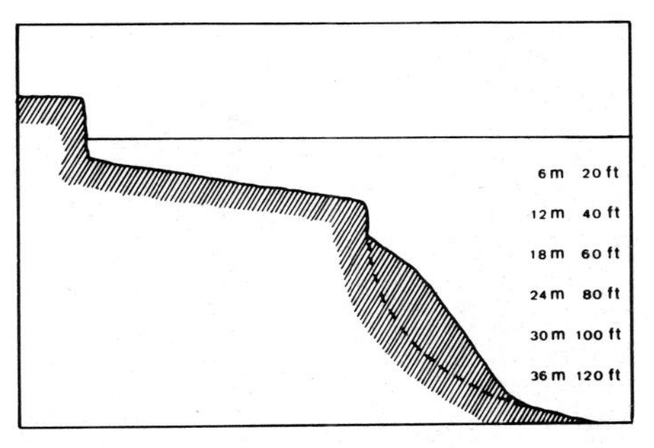


good turning point.
Going back shallow you can take a closer look at upper part of the buttresses (between 6 and 15 m - 20 and 50 ft). Mountainous Star Coral and lush gorgonians are typical of the drop-off zone here.
The *shallow terrace* (from 6 m - 20 ft - up) is marked by staghorn rubble, some Common Fans, Yellow Pencil Coral and small head corals.

Going *west* (right, facing the sea), you have the same buttress formation and a vertical wall, but the wall is deeper than east of the mooring. At its deepest the wall will start at 38 m (125 ft) and go down to 45 m (150 ft) with caves at the lower end. Otherwise the wall is very much like east with 'shallow' and 'deep' buttresses on both sides.
The lower parts of the sand valleys look like melting glaciers; they send a continuous sediment drizzle down the wall. The wall ends after a swim of about 20 min. This is a good turning point.
The buttresses continue all the way to Karpata and beyond.
On the *shallow terrace* just above the drop-off you find lush gorgonians. More shallow you have mainly a rubble bottom. Fairly close to the mooring you will see dead fragments of Elkhorn Coral covered by the Sun Anemone, a stinging anemone, as many as 100 per sq. m (10 per sq. ft) in places.

*Fish life.* The usual groupers and snappers can be seen along the reef slope here. On the shallow terrace close to the drop-off look for foraging goatfish and parrotfish.

An occasional Spiny Lobster is seen hiding in the lush soft coral/stony coral growths here. Also in the gorgonians you might see a pair of small filefish.

*Fig. 191*
*Dead Elkhorn Coral densely covered with Sun Anemones.*

# Dive site:
# **Karpata**

*Fig. 192*
*This large Common Sea Fan is being photographed by Ken Sherman.*

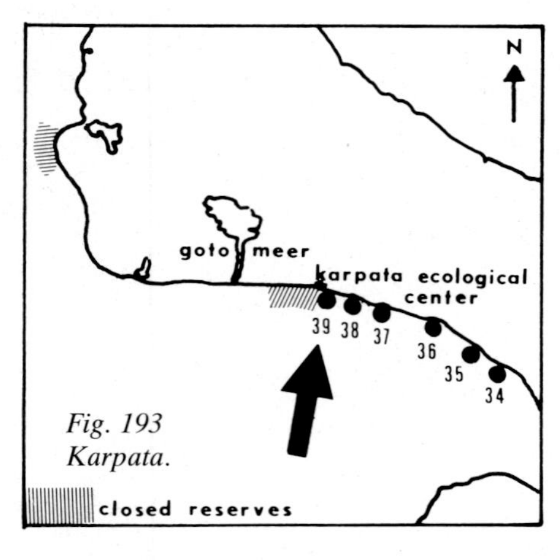


*Fig. 193*
*Karpata.*

1. *boat dive or shore dive*
2. *double barrel mooring / 3 m (10 ft); old anchor / 10 m (33 ft)*
3. *easy*
4. *50 m (167 ft)*
5. *all levels*
6. *9-10 m (30-33 ft)*
7. *very high*
8. *east (left, facing the sea); west of Karpata is a reserve closed for diving*
9. *30 m (100 ft)*
10. *limited snorkeling value.*

**Description**
You reach Karpata by driving north from town along the scenic road to Gotomeer until you get to the Karpata Ecological Center.
You can visit the coral reef exhibit here. The restoration of Karpata, an old plantation house, was finished in 1982; it serves now as the headquarters of the Netherlands Antilles National Parks Foundation (STINAPA) and also functions as a research station. On old maps Karpata is indicated as an anchorage. Ships used to call here to load plantation products.
They left several anchors on the reef, one of which is now used again as a permanent mooring. Those of you who know Karpata as a dive site from before 1975 should be prepared for a dramatic change of the shallow reef. A series of storms has caused the destruction of the Elkhorn Coral, and most of the large Common Sea Fans, for which Karpata was famous, have gone. But the reef slope is still beautiful, the steep buttresses and the tame fish being the main attractions.

From the shore you enter through a canal in the elkhorn barrier. The *shallow terrace* is narrow and almost devoid of coral growth down to 5 m (17 ft). Towards the drop-off you find a community of Mountainous Star Coral and gorgonians. Swim to the east (left, facing the sea) until you get to the old anchor at 10 m (33 ft). About 1 m (3 ft) deeper and a couple of meters further east lies another anchor, a bit more hidden. In the same area, but on the deep reef is a third one.
*Reef slope.* The buttresses have a very high coral cover and are extremely diverse. Large towers of Mountainous Star Coral, Giant Brain Coral and lush gorgonians decorate the upper reef slope. You will see plenty of black coral and a variety of sponges. The zone between 9 and 21 m (30 and 70 ft) is really the prettiest.
After some 10 min. to the east there is a deep 'canyon' and a steep buttress with a cave at 33 m (110 ft).
Return on the shallow terrace. In the 6-

*Fig. 194*
*Old anchor at Karpata.*

*Fig. 195*
*Black Durgon.*

9 m (20-30 ft) zone you will see a lot of excavation by grazers, Sergeant Major's nests and recolonization of dead coral limestone by the Encrusting Gorgonian. Above 6 m (20 ft) is staghorn rubble, large patches of Yellow Pencil Coral and abundant Corky Sea Finger.

*Fish life.* Yellowtail Snappers will gather around you as soon as you get near the drop-off. The Coneys are the most aggressive feeders, so be sure to bring some bread when you dive Karpata. Many Black Durgons are in the drop-off zone. There are Tiger- and Yellowmouth Groupers, and sometimes a small Marbled Grouper and a big Yellowfin Grouper are seen. Ocean Triggerfish and Horse-eye Jacks cruise in the blue water.

# Dive site:
# **Nukove** (Doblet)

*Fig. 196*
*Elkhorn barrier.*

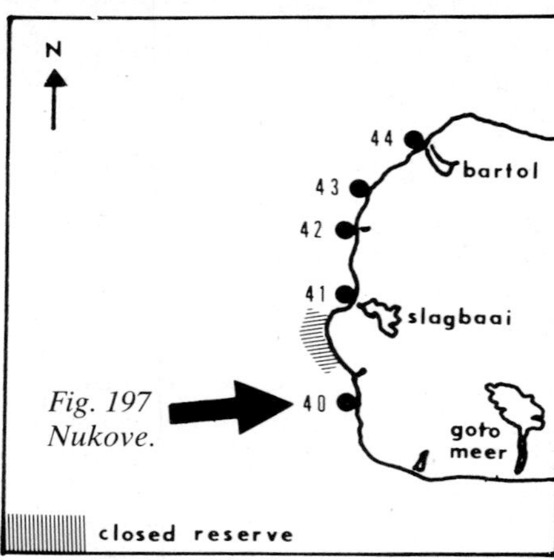


*Fig. 197*
*Nukove.*

1 *shore dive*
2 *planned*
3 *easy*
4 *90 m (300 ft)*
5 *all levels*
6 *10 m (33 ft)*
7 *fairly high (north, right facing the sea) to high (south) on buttresses*
8 *south (left, facing the sea) for SCUBA, north for snorkeling*
9 *27 m (90 ft)*
10 *very good snorkeling value.*

**Description**
Take the scenic road to Gotomeer and drive all the way to the barrier of the BOPEC (oil terminal) gate. Here the road turns right uphill and winds around the terminal. You pass Saliña Tam where cormorants can usually be seen, the old garbage dump and Boca Dreifi where the road sharply turns off the coast and back again to the shore. In between Boca Dreifi and Playa Frans, where the road ends, is only one track to the left shortly before you reach Playa Frans. That track leads to Nukove. If you miss it turn back at Playa Frans from where the track is a little easier to spot. Nukove is a very idyllic mini sand beach. Captain Don Stewart built a small concrete pier here. Be careful because the pier is washed at high tide and can be very slippery because of algae. To go diving you don't have to get onto the pier at all. You swim out through a channel cut in the elkhorn barrier next to the pier.

The *shallow terrace.* Note that the elk-

*Fig. 198*
*Tiger Grouper at a cleaning station. Large coral head is Giant Brain Coral.*

horn barrier only has living Elkhorn Coral at the surface and at the seaward edge. At low water spring-tide the whole barrier is exposed. Inside it is a massive framework of dead branches, tightly cemented together by pink crustose coralline algae. The Redlip Blenny is quite common on the dead elkhorn branches at the sides of the channel, and so is the Long-spined Sea Urchin. After leaving the channel you see some massive heads of Mountainous Star Coral, scattered Elkhorn Coral, fire corals and Leaf Coral. Further out the Staghorn Coral dominates down to a depth of 8 or 9 m (27-30 ft). To the north (right, facing the sea) the shallow terrace is particularly beautiful.
From shallow towards the drop-off you subsequently have: huge Elkhorn Coral, from 2 m (7 ft) to 4 m (13 ft), a zone with massive Mountainous Star Coral, all in 'knobby' form, a field of Staghorn Coral, and, just above the drop-off a mixed community of Yellow Pencil Coral, Staghorn Coral, Giant Brain Coral, Leaf Coral and fire corals. It is definitely recommended to spend the greater part of your dive above the drop-off or to go just snorkeling.

In the *drop-off* zone and along the upper *reef slope* are large towers of spherical Mountainous Star Coral, but mortality is fairly high. Buttresses are found to the *south* (left, facing the sea). There are gorgonians, sponges, crinoids and abundant black coral along the reef slope. Sheet and Scroll Corals dominate the *lower reef slope.*
Towards the *north* (right, facing the sea) there are some sand valleys, originating from reef slides, but no real buttresses. Small fishing boats frequently anchor with a stone in this area and cut the rope when the anchor gets stuck behind the coral. All these old ropes twisted around coral heads and gorgonians are not particularly decorative. Close to Playa Frans, after a swim of about 25 min., at 15 m (50 ft) is a Purple Tube Sponge with 51 (!) tubes.

*Fish life* includes big Barracuda, Tiger and Yellowmouth Groupers, big Bar Jacks, Many Creole Wrasses, Black Durgons, lots of Schoolmasters and big Yellowtail Snappers, Scrawled Filefish and many more.

Upon your return a metal stake at the entrance of the channel helps you to find directions.

# Dive site: **Boca Slagbaai**

*Fig. 199*
*Aerial view of Boca Slagbaai. Buildings from top to bottom: park warden's house, large storage building, former owner's house and manager's house. Arrow indicates the location of the old cannon.*

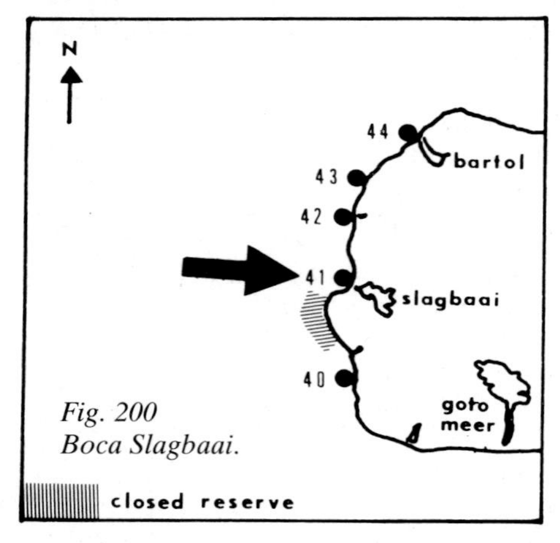


*Fig. 200*
*Boca Slagbaai.*

1. *Shore dive or boat dive*
2. *planned; anchoring in the sand (center of bay) permitted*
3. *normally easy, but less so with heavy surf*
4. *140 m (476 ft)*
5. *experienced, because of surf and ability for long swim required*
6. *9-10 m (30-33 ft)*
7. *fairly high*
8. *either way; directions rather different*
9. *27 m (90 ft)*
10. *good snorkeling value (north, right facing the sea)*

**Description**
To get here you drive to Rincon. From Rincon you follow the signs to Washingto Park. At the park entrance you will get a map. Follow the green arrows to Slagbaai If you are going out for a whole day, be sure to take some food and water.
Boca Slagbaai offers some fantastic diving as long as you don't make the mistake to swim straight out and down in the center of the bay. Slagbaai used to be an importan anchorage for ships that carried salt, aloe, goats, charcoal and divi-divi seed pods to Curaçao. It was so important that there even was a customs office: the house in th very right (facing the sea) corner of the bay, now occupied by one of the park wardens. Perhaps because of the anchorag the bay itself is rather barren and the reef slope in front of the bay somewhat degraded. That's why we recommend diving either north or south of the bay and warn you to be prepared for a long swim if you want to see the good things without accumulating too much bottom time. Moorings are planned both on the north and the south side of Slagbaai, so for the more exploratory-minded we will describe two dives: Slagbaai to Wayaka, and Slagbaai-south (fig. 201).

**Slagbaai to Wayaka**
Enter in the central-right part of the bay (just right of the largest building) and snorkel out slightly to the right. At a depth of 4,5 - 5 m (15-17 ft), in a straight line with the front wall of the park warden's

*ig. 201*
*Detailed map of Boca Slagbaai and Waya-*
*a, showing the location of the buttresses.*

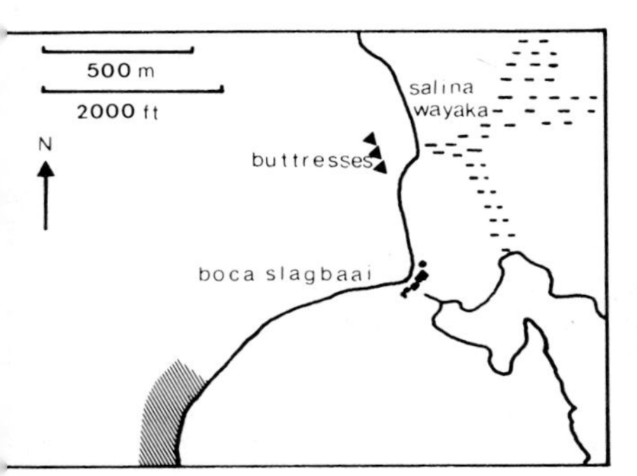


*Fig. 202*
*Field of Mountainous Star Coral in knobby columnar form.*

ouse, you will see six cannon, partly uried in the sand and an old anchor hain. An ancient wreck? No, don't be ooled like the Dutch geologist who crossed he Atlantic in a small yacht all by himself, ast anchor at Slagbaai and decided his nchor could have no better hold than ehind those old cannon. Until he dove own to discover that the cannon were ake, concrete replicas, halves to suggest hey were buried in the sand and put there n 1974 for the shooting of the film 'Sharks Treasure'. Continue to snorkel north (to he right) and towards the *drop-off* until ou have the large tumbled-down rock at he northern entrance of the bay and the ide-front window of the warden's house n a straight line. This is about the place to egin your dive.
Don't go deep, save bottom time for the ast part of the dive (as described here, it is a 75 min. dive!). Initially, mortality among he corals is rather high but after about 20 min. the reef slope becomes more attractive. After another 10 min. north you get to a very conspicuously protruding buttress, followed by a deeply cut valley and several more buttresses with alternating valleys. This area probably represents the best example of buttress formation on Bonaire. The first buttress is just south of the rubble wall of the Salina Wayaka, the sixth right off the center of it (fig. 201). The buttresses are near-vertical in places and quite impressive. Resist any temptation to explore the deep reef: it continues down to 60 or 70 m (200-230 ft)! On your way to the buttresses you may see a big Green Moray Eel, several large Tiger Groupers and many Yellowmouth Groupers, White-spotted Filefish, Barracuda, Schoolmasters, abundant Creole Wrasses, and, in the buttress area, a school of Tarpon.
Return shallow over a field of Staghorn Coral that extends down to 7 m (23 ft). When you approach Slagbaai again you have large heads of Mountainous Star Coral at a depth of about 4 m (13 ft), Leaf Coral, Club Finger Coral and Elkhorn Coral. This area is recommended for snorkeling too!

**Slagbaai-south**
Enter in the southernmost (left) corner of the bay from the little sand beach near the cave in the cliff. Keep close to the cliff and to the left. The lower edge of the cliff consists of some living Elkhorn Coral and

*Fig. 203*
*Old cannon at the base of the cliff.*

*Fig. 204*
*View of the houses at Boca Slagbaai from the point where you begin your dive.*

fire coral, and encrusted dead coral limestone, partly covered with the Encrusting Colonial Anemone. Just before you reach a partly exposed large rock that broke off the cliff you can see two cannon in 1 m (3 ft) depth. These cannon are real, and blending in perfectly with the environment because they are covered with purplish crustose coralline algae, just like the cliff itself.
Their presence was first reported in 1981 by Ralph Nolen, a tugboat captain on Bonaire, whom we were able to keep from salvaging the cannon only by the promise that he would be mentioned in this book as the finder of the cannon. This promise we gladly keep, because they are the only old cannon on Bonaire that can be seen by anyone who is able to swim and breathe through a snorkel. They originate from a small fort on the cliff above.
From the cannon you then snorkel out towards the drop-off, taking a south-west course. You will swim over a coral community of Leaf Coral, Club Finger Coral and Mountainous Star Coral, alternated with sand-rubble. Near the *drop-off* you will see massive heads of Mountainous Star Coral. You start your dive when the central house begins to disappear behind the cliff (fig. 204).
Large coral structures abound on the *upper slope,* but coral cover is low on the lower slope. Towards the south (left) the slope is very steep in places with abundant Cavernous Star Coral. We recommend that you spend the greater part of your dive more shallow than 18 m (60 ft). Here you will see impressive towers of Mountainous Star Coral, both in roof shingle and in knobby formations. You will also see big Tiger Groupers, Yellowmouth Grouper, perhaps a Yellowfin- and a Nassau Grouper, Barracuda, Schoolmaster, Horse-eye Jacks and, in the drop-off zone, Black Durgons. Return shallows, at 9 m (30 ft) or less, after about 30 min. The reef above the drop-off is like a fairy tale: a dense cover of Mountainous Star Coral, in colors ranging from almost grass-green to tan and purplish-grey, both in knobby and in smooth spherical forms.

*Fig. 205*
*Shallow terrace at Slagbaai-south: Mountainous Star Coral in smooth spherical and knobby columnar form.*

*Fig. 206*
*Profile of the shallow terrace and the drop-off zone at Slagbaai-south; at the base of the cliff is a sandy channel with big limestone blocks.*

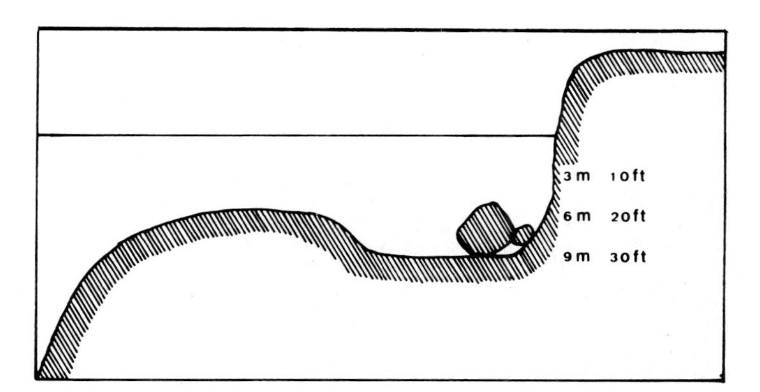

*Fig. 207*
*At the base of the cliff you can find galleries formed by huge limestone blocks.*

The reef is virgin in appearance. Some of the big coral heads demonstrate the burrowing and grazing activity of other reef invertebrates. In between and under the large coral heads you find a variety of other coral species and gorgonians and some lobster too.

On the *shallow terrace* you will not find the usual zone of Staghorn Coral. The extensive field of Mountainous Star Coral reaches up to 6 or 7 m (20 or 23 ft) and is followed shoreward by a sand channel at a depth of 9 m (30 ft), (fig. 206).
In the sand channel are huge gorgonians, some Staghorn Coral and small head corals.

In the channel you will also see large blocks of limestone that broke off the cliff and tumbled down into the ocean.
Unter the ledges made by these limestone blocks you are likely to see snappers and an occasional, very large, Porcupine Fish. The cliff wall is covered with gorgonians (Common Sea Fan is quite abundant), some Elkhorn Coral, fire corals, brain corals and encrusting coralline algae. As you get closer to the entrance of Slagbaai the sand channel becomes less outspoken and you will see more Leaf Coral and Club Finger Coral on the shallow terrace.

# Dive site:
# **Playa Funchi**

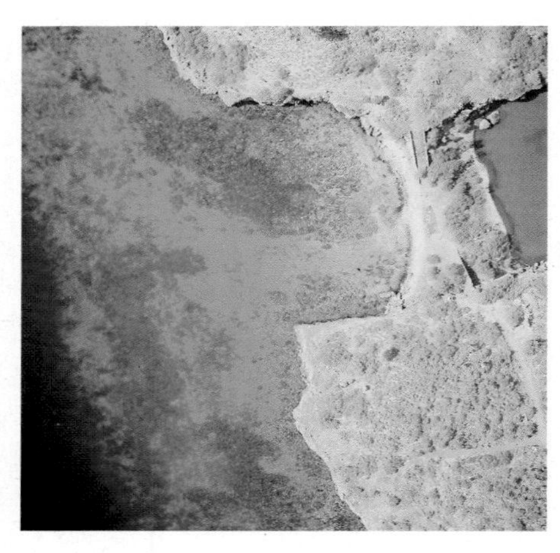

*Fig. 208*
*Aerial view of Playa Funchi.*

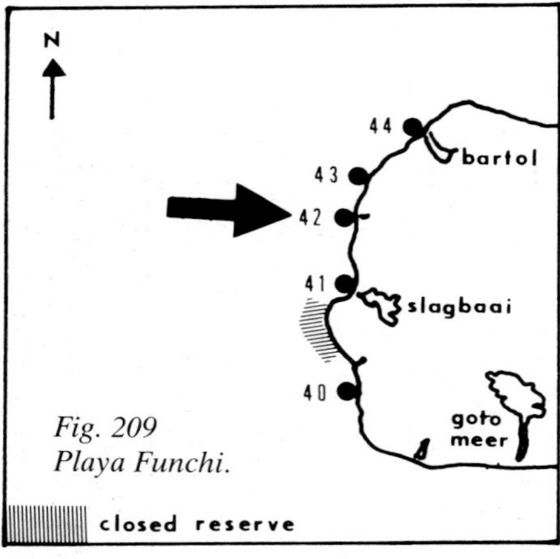


*Fig. 209*
*Playa Funchi.*

1 *shore dive*
2 —
3 *easy*
4 *130 m (430 ft)*
5 *all levels*
6 *11-12 m (37-40 ft)*
7 *fairly high*
8 *either way*
9 *27 m (90 ft)*
10 *good snorkeling value (northern part of bay)*

**Description**
The most popular snorkeling area for visitors to Washington-Slagbaai Park. See Slagbaai (no. 41) for driving directions. Inside the Park you can follow either the green or the yellow arrows. Enter next to the remnants of a man-made pier and swim towards the drop-off over the sandy central section of the bay.

The *shallow terrace* is fairly wide and shows an extensive field of Staghorn Cora down to about 9 m (30 ft) in the center of the bay. Close to the drop-off is a narrow zone with Mountainous Star Coral. Some large heads of Mountainous Star Coral are present on the *upper reef slope;* otherwise the slope is varied but has no distinct zonation. Sponges are present and of the black corals only the Pinnate Black Coral is here. North of Playa Funchi and along Bonaire's north coast the other species, the Dichotomous Black Coral, that is mostly used for jewelry making, is absent. Returning from a dive to the *south* (left, facing the sea) you head back into the bay above the drop-off: there is a very pretty coral community of Mountainous Star Coral, Leaf Coral, fire corals and Yellow Pencil Coral, similar to the one at Knife (no. 24).
Closer to the cliff is knobby Mountainous Star Coral and Elkhorn Coral in an otherwise sandy strip along the edge of the cliff. To the *north* the reef slope is initially quite similar to south, but gradually more gorgonians appear and mortality among stony corals is higher. Again return over the shallow terrace. Just above the drop-off Mountainous Star Coral is the dominant species. Towards the shore there is in places a rather barren zone with coral rubble, some Staghorn Coral and Pillar Coral. Further inshore you find the community that is characteristic for a steep cliff coast: big blocks of limestone broken off the cliff, some Elkhorn Coral, lots of fire coral, extensive cover by crustose coralline algae and numerous Common Sea Fans. As you turn back into the bay from the northern side you have extensive

Fig. 210
*Pinnate Black Coral.*

ields of Mountainous Star Coral in knobby orm, together with Leaf Coral and fire corals from 6 to 3 m (20 to 10 ft). Some coral mounds reach a few meters (6 to 10 ft) high. From 3 to 1 m (10 to 3 ft) you ind a beautiful Leaf Coral-fire coral ommunity, and finally Elkhorn Coral, eaching up to the surface. In the center of he bay, on the northern side of the en-rance channel is a huge colony of Smooth Brain Coral that is exposed at low tide. The northern half of the bay and the hallow terrace outside and north of the bay are a must for snorkelers.

*Fish life.* Creole Wrasses and Creole Fish are abundant as are the Yellowtail Snap-pers and Schoolmasters. Large Bar Jacks and Ocean Triggerfish are often seen here. You may also see big Yellowfin Groupers, a shy Nassau Grouper of over one meter (over 3,5 ft) and a Southern Stingray. There are fairly big Rock Hinds, White-potted Filefish and, in the shallow central part of the bay, Midnight Parrotfish and a pair of French Angelfish.

Fig. 211
*Mixed shallow water coral community at Playa Funchi. Divers: Franklin Winklaar and Doug Daniels.*

# Dive site:
# **Playa Bengé**

*Fig. 212*
*Aerial view of the spurs and grooves at Playa Bengé.*

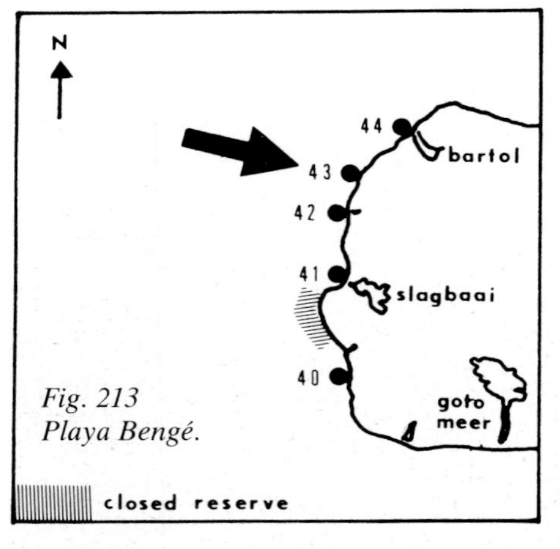


*Fig. 213*
*Playa Bengé.*

1 *shore dive*
2 —
3 *sometimes difficult due to surf*
4 *120 m (400 ft)*
5 *experienced (because of entry and possible current)*
6 *10 m (33 ft)*
7 *high (upper reef slope) to moderate (lower reef slope)*
8 *north (right, facing the sea); see reef map*
9 *45 m (150 ft)*
10 *very good snorkeling value.*

**Description**
This is a 'Bonaire special' located in Washington-Slagbaai Park. When we first dove Bengé we wouldn't even talk about it to others. Its special features are the large number of big groupers encountered here, a beautiful array of spurs and grooves in shallow water and a fairy-tale-like wall and cave for those who feel comfortable at making a deep dive.
But also: a - sometimes - rough entry, possible strong current and carrying all your gear through a partly flooded saliña in the rainy season. So if you mostly enjoy the relaxed boat dives, forget about Bengé Bengé is for the adventurous, exploratory-minded and experienced diver.
For directions see Slagbaai (no. 41). Inside the Park follow the yellow arrows. Always ask the warden at the park entrance if you can safely drive into the saliña. Even if it looks dry and even if you have a 4-wheel drive jeep your car can get stuck. The park wardens frequently put a cactus barrier at the end of the road. This does not mean that you can't dive Bengé, but you will have to carry your gear to the shore.
You enter the water in the center of the bay, right where you climb over the coral rubble wall. Swim out almost perpendicular to the beach, keeping a huge Smooth Brain Coral at your right and subsequently swimming over beautifully wave-adapted Elkhorn Coral. Swimming to the north (right facing the sea), the *shallow terrace* offers a series of most interesting 'spurs and grooves' (fig. 214 and 222).
The spurs are composed of Elkhorn Coral, many of which are dead and overgrown by crustose coralline algae, brain corals, fire corals, the Encrusting Colonial Anemone, the Common Sea Fan and Leaf Coral. On the deeper limits of the spurs there are numerous Long-spined Sea Urchins and many excavated coral structures testify to the grazing habits of these urchins.

Amongst the *fishes,* that are abundant you should notice the Jewelfish (juvenile of the Yellowtail Damselfish), especially between the plates of the fire coral and the

*Fig. 214*
*Reef map of the spurs and grooves at Playa Bengé.*

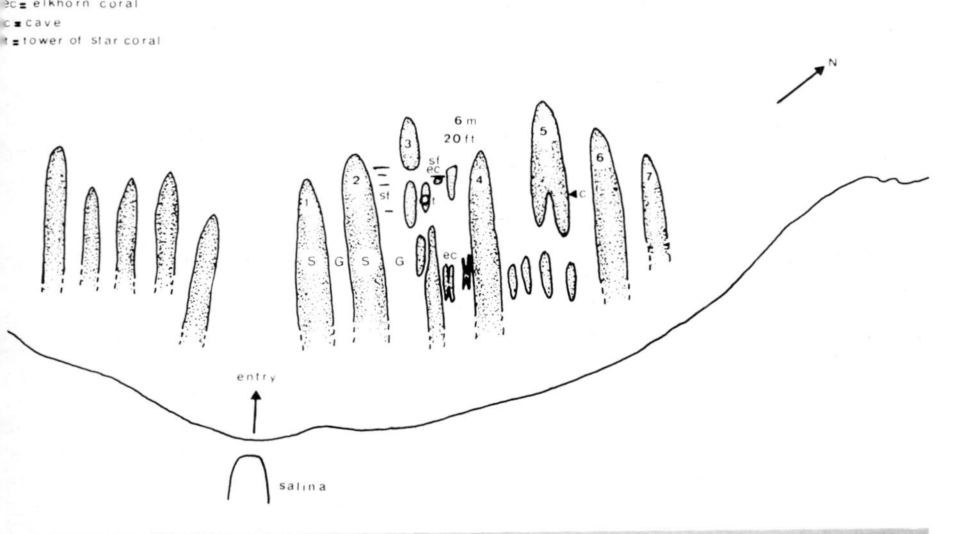

*Fig. 215*
*The Common Sea Fan is characteristic of areas with strong water movement.*

Fig. 216
*Deepwater Gorgonians.*

Leaf Coral, the Sergeant Major, the Redlip Blenny, particularly on the dead overgrown corals, numerous Brown Chromis, the Bluestriped Grunt, Mahogany Snapper, and, in the shadow of the overhanging ridges, the Glassy Sweeper. Also you shouldn't be surprised to find a Nurse Shark resting in the shelter of one of the spurs.

As you get to the 5th spur you should look for some big Tiger Groupers; on the northern side of that spur a huge Nassau Grouper resides in a cave. But in a group of divers only the first will see the grouper, because it retreats into its quarters as more people appear at the front door.

When you are determined to take a look at the reef slope or make the deep dive, you snorkel towards the drop-off and to the north (right, facing the sea) for 10 to 15 min. before you begin the descent (otherwise you will accumulate too much bottom-time for the deep wall).

The *upper reef slope* has a carpet of Mountainous Star Coral and Giant Brain Coral. Deepwater Gorgonians (Schramm's Iciligorgia), characteristic for strong currents, are common here.

A sand terrace begins at 25 m (83 ft). Further north the sand terrace is at 33 m (110 ft), bends seaward and is followed by a second drop-off. The sand terrace then narrows and becomes continuous with the reef slope that is getting steeper (45°) at this point (for bearings at the surface, you are now almost at the cape at the northern end of the bay). Now follow the slope down to 40 m (133 ft) and you will see a vertical wall down to 48 m (160 ft) where the sand terrace starts again.

The wall and the cave in it are covered with yellow and white sponges, Purple Tube Sponges, Tub Sponges, reddishpurple Deepwater Gorgonians, Black Wire Corals and pink 'black corals'. Truly a fairy tale. But your bottom-time is limited

If there is a current to the north you must be very careful, but there is no reason to panic because you return shallow over the spurs and grooves where there will be no current. For those who don't want to make the deep dive: the reef slope between

Fig. 217
*Nurse Shark resting under a ledge.*

10 and 21 m (30 and 70 ft) is just as beautiful.

*Fish life* is spectacular. There are always big groupers, although you may not always see all species on each dive. Over at least a dozen dives we have recorded big Nassau Groupers, Marbled Groupers, big Yellowfin Groupers, and many Tiger Groupers, Southern Stingrays, schools of over a hundred Horse-eye Jacks and a Nurse Shark, to name only the most spectacular things.

One final remark: don't go south (left, facing the sea). The reef is far less attractive and quite eroded by grazers (the number of Long-spined Sea Urchins is incredible).

# Dive site:
# **Boca Bartól**

*Fig. 218*
*Spurs and grooves at Boca Bartól. Diver: Habitat Dive Master David Serlin.*

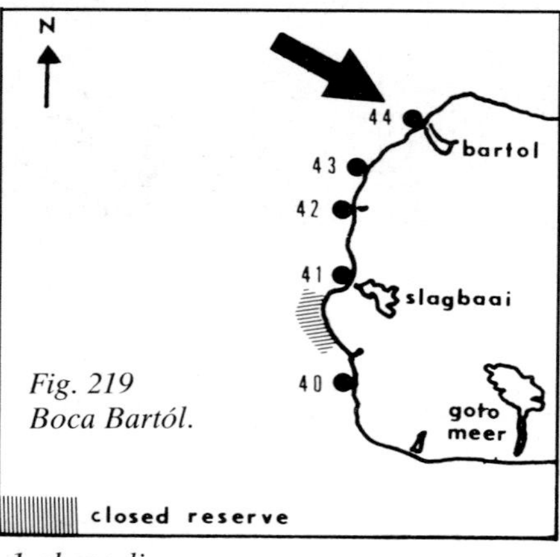


*Fig. 219*
*Boca Bartól.*

1 *shore dive*
2 —
3 *often difficult because of surf*
4 *150 m (500 ft)*
5 *highly experienced (rough entry, currents, deep dive) for the northern entrance; experienced (sometimes rough entry, currents) for southern entrance*
6 *11-12 m (37-40 ft)*
7 *moderate*
8 *two separate dives from the northern and southern entrance of the bay (see reef map)*
9 *48 m (160 ft), north; 24 m (80 ft), south*
10 *good snorkeling value when sea is calm.*

**Description**
As a general rule we have described dive sites that are accessible to the vast majority of divers. Therefore we feel entitled to making a few exceptions to this rule and Boca Bartól is one of them. It is another 'Bonaire Special' but reserved only to the more adventurous and experienced diver. On numerous occasions we have stood ashore at Bartól, looked at the sea and the waves, argued over 'yes or no' and finally put the trip off. You should do the same and, if you don't feel completely at ease, don't dive Bartól but go to Playa Funchi, Playa Bengé or Slagbaai instead. It is located in Washington - Slagbaai Park. For directions we refer you to Slagbaai (nr. 41). Inside the park you follow the yellow arrows.
We describe two separate dives: one from the northern corner of the bay, the other from the southern corner.

**The northern entrance**
We describe a - fascinating - deep dive, which doesn't mean of course that you *have to make* a deep dive. Park your car at the northern end of the bay and investigate the point of entry first: it is in the northern (right, facing the sea) corner of the bay. Swim through the surf in between the two large rocks, keeping the third rock to your right. Keep a slight left course towards the

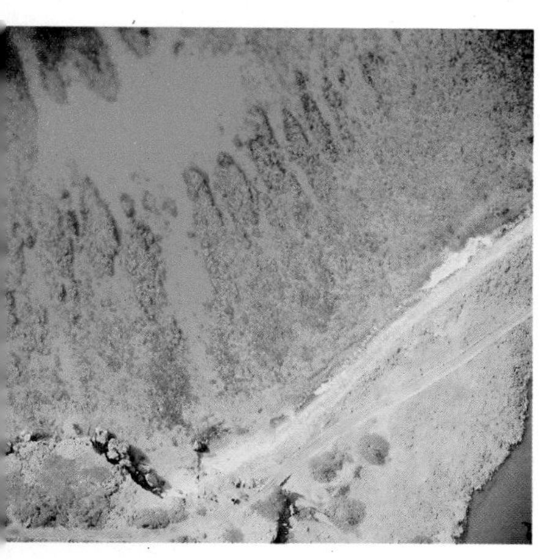

*Fig. 220*
*Aerial photograph of spurs and grooves at Boca Bartól.*

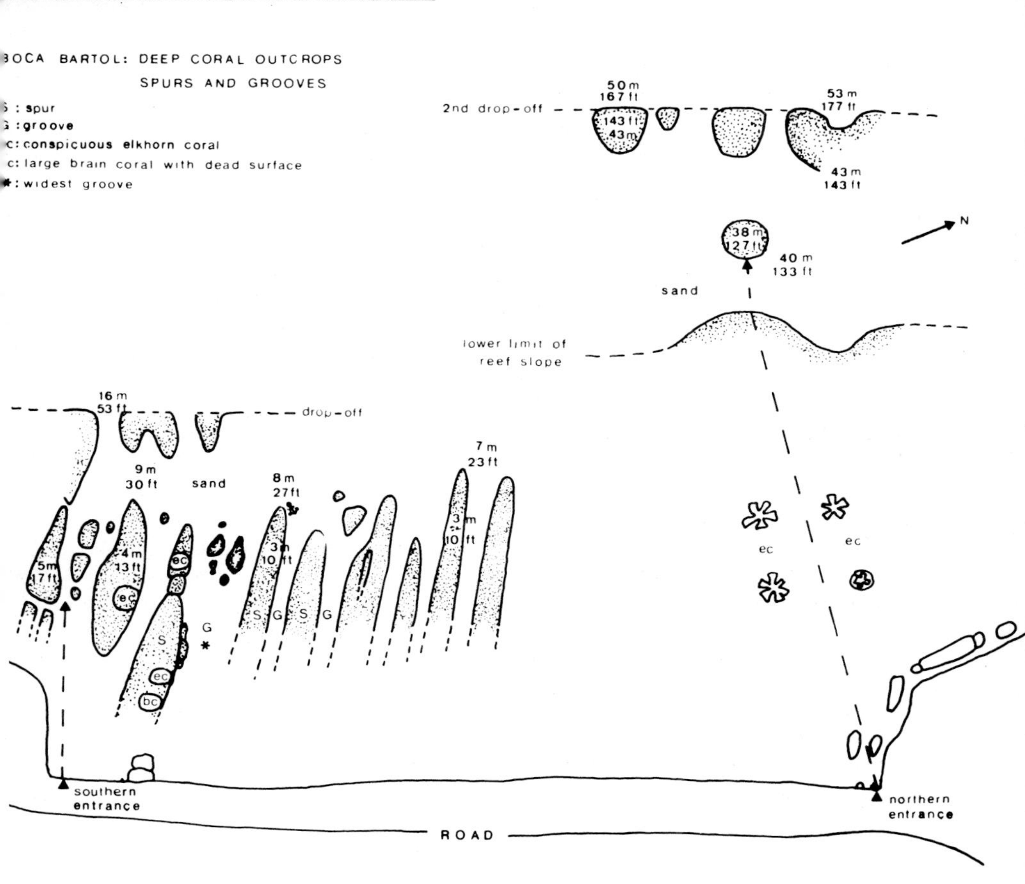


*Fig. 221*
*Reef map of Boca Bartól.*

*Fig. 222*
*Spurs and grooves are coral ridges with alternating sand channels that develop in shallow areas with strong water movements.*

drop-off (fig. 221). Bearings on your way to the drop-off are a high Elkhorn Coral, like a statue on a pedestal of dead coral, that you should keep to your right and a larger but lower Elkhorn Coral on your left. Next seaward are two large, flattened Elkhorn Corals. You pass in between. Try to keep the same course, still snorkeling, all the way past the drop-off until you lose the bottom out of sight. Then go down to 10 to 15 m (33 to 50 ft), as shallow as possible to save bottom-time, but deep enough to be able to see the bottom while you swim out into the blue. When you feel that a current is displacing you quickly to the north, turn back and make a shallow dive. If not, continue for 3 to 5 minutes from the moment that you are over the sand bottom. You should then see a dark spot on the bottom, the first of five coral outcrops that we're heading for. Time to go down to the bottom.
The face of the first coral outcrop is at 38 m (127 ft); further out and to the left is a second one at 43 m (143 ft) and from there you will see the other three outcrops to the right. They are about 10-15 m (33-50 ft) across. The coral islands are so fascinating that you might like to spend an hour there, but even with 15 minutes bottom-time you have to make a stop of 1 minute at 6 m (20 ft) and 4 minutes at 3 m (10 ft). Keep a close look at your watch and your pressure gauge. Decide to return once more to Boca Bartól rather than taking any unnecessary risks.
Within the short time available you may see large Tiger Groupers, Nassau Grouper Yellowfin Grouper, Dog Snapper, Southern Stingray, perhaps a school of over a hundred Horse-eye Jacks and a school of Ocean Triggerfish. It is so overwhelming (with a little bit of nitrogen narcosis added that you just don't know where to look. You could just as well leave your camera ashore on a first dive to Boca Bartól because you will only have time to look. The southernmost isle at 43 m (143 ft) has a seaward ledge with beautiful sponges, deep reddish gorgonians and pink 'black corals'. The northernmost, kidney-shaped outcrop has a cave at its seaward edge, apparently

he hiding place for both the big Nassau Grouper, the Yellowfin Grouper and the snappers.
Don't expect to see all of this in one dive, but you will certainly want to come back. If you want to make the most out of this dive, ascend straight up from the islands to 6 m (20 ft) and make your first stop while heading back towards the shore, taking the reef slope below as a guide.

**The southern entrance**
You swim out from the southernmost (left) corner of the bay. Most of the time entering here presents no real problem. Soon after you have gone through the surf you will see the spurs and grooves that are characteristic of the *shallow terrace* on this side of the bay (fig. 222 and 221). To the north (right, facing the sea) they extend to the center of the bay, to the south they continue well outside the bay. Take along the waterproof reef map to guide you through the labyrinth of galleries. The spurs are quite well developed and covered with Leaf Coral, fire corals, Elkhorn Coral and crustose coralline algae. Encrusting Colonial Anemones spread like a carpet over the coral limestone and Common Sea Fans decorate the spurs.
Near the tip of the spur just north of the widest groove (indicated on the map with an asterisk) lies a small old anchor. It is cemented to an isolated head of Cavernous Star Coral, just seaward of the tip of that spur, and partly buried in the sand.

Seaward of the spurs and grooves is a barren sand flat that extends almost to the drop-off. In the *drop-off zone* opposite the point of entry you find some eroded coral patches. Two sand rivers flow down the reef slope in between those coral patches. There are some large towers of Mountainous Star Coral just below the drop-off, but generally you will see a lot of toppled and eroded coral heads along the *reef slope*. Mountainous- and Cavernous Star Coral are the most abundant coral species there. In addition gorgonians and sponges are common, and on the deeper part of the slope some big Pinnate Black Coral occurs. The reef slope leaves a desolate, though exciting impression. The deep sand terrace starts at 21-24 m (70-80 ft) just to the right and left of the sand rivers, but the reef slope quickly reaches deeper, down to 33-43 m (100-130 ft), as you go further north or south of the sand rivers.
*Fish life.* You can expect to see some big groupers here, like Tiger-, Yellowmouth- and Yellowfin Groupers, but also Gray Snappers, Ocean Triggerfish and Black Durgons. You are likely to see the Southern Stingray, both on the shallow and the deep sand terrace, and you shouldn't be surprised to see the majestic Spotted Eagle Ray, a big Barracuda, or a Nurse Shark resting under a ledge at the base of one of the spurs. In very shallow water there are Midnight and Rainbow Parrotfish.

*Fig. 223*
*Common Sea Fans decorate the spurs.*

# Stinging animals

There are no animals on the reef that will attack divers out of aggression. However, some will defend themselves when touched or stepped on. You will surely meet with the Longspined Sea Urchin or the fire corals sooner or later.
Therefore it is good to be aware of a few animals that can sting or otherwise cause a painful sensation.

**Do-not-touch-me Sponge**
Its name alone should contain a sufficient warning. When touched with bare hands its needle-sharp spicules will damage your skin and cause a burning, itching sensation that may last for a few days in serious cases. Spicules imbedded in a wetsuit or gloves can be transferred to bare skin, too. There is nothing you can do about it except prevent it: hands off!

**Coelenterates.** Most coelenterates have nematocysts that, when fired, will penetrate your skin and release a small quantity of poison. The most common sting is that of the fire coral. It causes a painful, burning sensation, but the effects will normally have disappeared without treatment within a few hours. More serious are the stings of certain Jellyfish and Seawasps. You will often not notice the animal that has stung you. Leave the water as soon as possible and remove any tentacles that may be left on the affected area. Apply alcohol, dilute ammonia or meat tenderizer. If serious symptoms occur, such as cramps or difficulty in breathing, see a doctor immediately.
The Portuguese Man-of-war, whose stings can cause very serious symptoms, is hardly ever seen on Bonaire.

**Sea urchins** 'You haven't experienced Bonaire if you haven't stepped on the Long-spined Sea Urchin'. Whether you will appreciate the joke if you actually do step on one remains in doubt, because it *is* painful. To try and remove the spines of the Long-spined Sea Urchin is a waste of time.
Apply vinager to dissolve the spines or simply endure a little more pain and beat the wounded area with a smooth stone to powder the spines, so that they dissolve more rapidly.
The pain usually disappears within one or two hours and recovery will be complete within a few days. The risk of an infection is negligible. You are less likely to step into the small, thick-spined, Rock-boring Urchin that is hidden in small crevices in the rocks. If you do, however, try to remove the spines because they will not readily dissolve and may cause infection.

*Fig. 224*
*Do-not-touch-me Sponge.*

*Fig. 225*
*The tentacles of the fire coral contain nematocysts which penetrate the skin upon contact.*

**Fire Worm.** Never pick up a Fire Worm! It has bristle-like appendages that will penetrate into the skin and release a venom, causing an itching, burning sensation. If you have touched a Fire Worm, try to remove any bristles that are left in the skin with sticky tape and apply alcohol or diluted ammonia.

**Scorpionfish.** The Scorpionfish is so well-camouflaged that it can be easily stepped on by swimmers or inadvertently touched by a diver looking for a holdfast. Its spines penetrate the skin and a venom is secreted. Severe pain can result. See a doctor as soon as possible.

We emphasize: all of these animals act in SELF-DEFENSE. Urchins don't leap up off the bottom to stab people; Fire Worms won't crawl up on you and attack. Divers with good buoyancy control who place their hands carefully on coral rock and keep their bodies up off the bottom, will solve two problems: first they won't be stung or spined, and second they won't damage the living marine animals. By protecting yourself with appropriate buoyancy control, you also protect the reef.

*Fig. 227*
*Fire Worm preying on gorgonian.*

*Fig. 226*
*Long-spined Sea Urchin.*

*Fig. 228*
*Camouflaged head of a Spotted Scorpionfish.*

# Night diving

Divers who restrict their undersea excursions to daylight hours miss a very special facet of the undersea world. Many of the reef's creatures are nocturnal, so diurnal divers can only observe nighttime animals while they sleep, if they see them at all. No dive vacation is complete without at least one night dive.

Some words of caution, however: nighttime diving requires a higher level of diving skill than daytime diving. Divers with poor buoyancy control often bounce off the reef (which is terrible for the coral, of course), or use their hands for sculling to stay above the bottom. In the night time contact with the reef usually results in contact with Long-spined Sea Urchins, not a very comfortable situation (the urchins don't like it either!). And 'sculling' becomes impossible at night because one hand must hold the light. Divers wishing to practice for a night dive should carry a light throughout a day dive and pay careful attention to buoyancy control.

It is recommended that each diver have at least one light (I dive with three); trying to see by someone else's light is difficult and frustrating. Since most Bonaire night dives are from shore, some divers bring one or two chemical light sticks to mark their paths.

Finally, before you enter the water look for clear, cup-shaped jellyfish with four tentacles: Caribbean sea wasps. These animals can give a painful sting and should be avoided. They are not seen often on Bonaire, however, and when they do show up are usually in waters 5 m (15 ft) or shallower.

Why is a night dive worth all this preparation?

Ah! We're so glad you asked!

There is a 'changing of the guard' from daytime to nighttime on the reef. Nocturnal fish, the big-eyed fish, hide in the daytime but emerge at night: cardinalfish, squirrelfish, soldierfish. Most of the fish you see in the daytime will be sleeping at night: small groupers lean against rocks or rest inside sponges; Creole Fish sleep in the tops of coral heads; tiny Sharpnose Puffers cuddle into depressions on the sides of sponges or around the Orange Tube Corals. Look for familiar fish with new colorations: Creole Fish turn to mottled colorations at night; Blue Tangs acquire vertical stripes. Occasionally you'll find a parrotfish snoozing within a mucous cocoon: apparently the cocoon helps prevent nighttime predators like Moray Eels, from scenting the parrotfish.

If disturbed, sleeping fish will flee the disturbance, often swimming into urchins or coral heads. That is why we ask you to try not to disturb the fish at night. No one enjoys being stabbed by a sea urchin, especially in the middle of a deep sleep! Invertebrates take over the nighttime reef

*Fig. 229*
*Orange Tube Coral.*

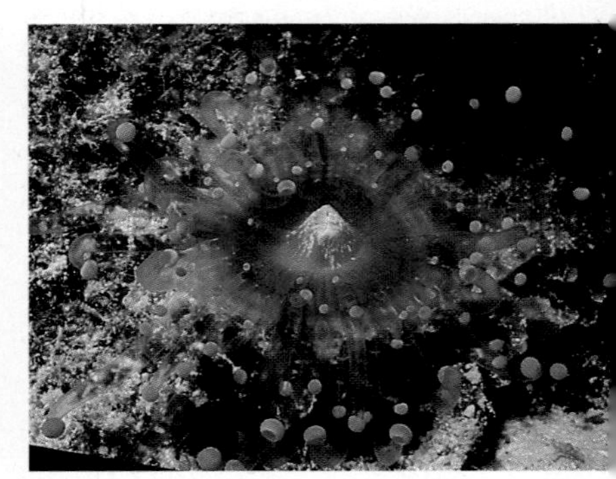

*Fig. 230*
*Coral-like anemone* Pseudocorynactis caribbeorum.

You might not even recognize some of the familiar corals as their polyps extend for feeding; their entire appearance is changed. Brain coral becomes fuzzy, Flower Coral polyps are so long they look almost like anemones, and the dull Orange Tube Corals blossom at night with incredibly lovely orange 'flowers'. You'll see at least two anemones that aren't 'out' in the daytime at all: the most beautiful is an almost transparent animal with a tiny bright orange 'ball' at the tip of each tentacle. It belongs to the so-called 'Coral-like anemones' and has only recently been named *Pseudocorynactis caribbeorum*. Approach is gently; at the least disturbance it folds its arms inside itself and transforms into a brown lump. Bonaire's other nocturnal anemone is a tube anemone. You'll see it on the sand, and if you disturb it - zip! it disappears into its tube.

The mollusks, very shy in the daytime, come out to hunt at night. If you're lucky, you may see one of several species of octopus that live on Bonaire's reefs. You're more likely to see a foraging nudibranch (a snail without a shell) or even a shelled mollusk like a Music Volute or the beautiful Flame Helmet, though. Please remember that Bonaire's reefs are protected: feast your eyes on the nocturnal beauties, take photographs, enjoy, and leave the animals on the reef.

The crustaceans come out at night, too. You'll see a pair of bright reflectors of your light in a coral crevice. Look more closely, and you'll realize that the reflectors are the eyes of a pink shrimp. Banded Coral Shrimp leave their hide-aways at night. Every crevice seems to contain encrusted shells inhabited by red-bodied, blue-eyed hermit crabs.
Arrow crabs hunt actively at night, sometimes by perching in the branches of the soft corals. If you are observant - and lucky - you may spot a Spiny Lobster or even an uncommon Shovelnosed Lobster, tiptoeing on the nightly hunt.

Of course, Long-spined Sea Urchins seem to be everywhere at night; as they leave their daytime nooks to forage they become powerful incentives to good buoyancy control. Find a sandy area with no urchins, settle down, and turn off your lights. Your eyes will quickly adjust to the darkness, and you'll realize that you can see - not details, but large shapes - quite well. If you had lost your light on this dive you could have easily and safely swum in to shore. (Some people enjoy night diving with no light; instead of watching the animals they enjoy the sensation of sensory deprivation, of floating.) Now, wave your hand in the dark water: the disturbance causes all the tiny bioluminescent creatures to light up in a display of underwater fireworks.

On one dive, you probably won't see all the sights mentioned here, but you might see all these and more. Go quietly into the dark sea, move gently, look carefully: a new world awaits you at night underwater.

# Fish feeding

*Fig. 231*
*The author trying to feed 'D'Artagnan'.*

One of the simplest ways to feel more comfortable in the underwater world and to lure fish closer for observation and/or photography is by feeding the fish. Bonaire's waters are ideal for this activity.

The easiest fish food to obtain is bread, but since it immediately breaks up in the water bread has two disadvantages: firstly it clouds the water and secondly it will attract mobs of 'Bonairean attack yellow-tails' who, frenzied by the crumbs floating around, will nip at anything that looks like it might be food: fingertips, ear lobes, exhaust bubbles, etc.

Some alternatives to bread are hot dogs or vienna sausages, chees, or even a banana. These foods don't cloud the water, and they are easy for a diver to handle and control. We advise you to carry the food in a can (such as a peanut can) instead of a plastic bag (fish rip bags apart). Wear gloves to protect your hands. When you're ready to begin feeding, settle down on a rubble bottom or even the mooring; you won't have to worry about buoyancy control and you won't be damaging living coral.

Break a little of the food into the water so the fish know you're feeding, then just hold up the food and let the fish nibble away. Among the fish you'll attract will be Yellowtail Snappers, a variety of parrot-fish, small groupers, French Angelfish, Spanish Hogfish. Remember, the more food scattered or 'chummed' in the water, the more uncontrollable the Yellowtail mobs become. Enjoy!

| ;ood fish 'eeding sites | *Fishes you're likely to attract:* | |
|---|---|---|
| | *in the blue water* | *near the mooring* |
| Carl's Hill (no. 21) | Yellowtail Snappers | Coneys, Graysbys, parrotfish |
| ferry's Jam/ Ebo's Special (no. 22) | Yellowtail Snappers | A great variety of little fish: parrotfish, grunts, goatfish, wrasses, etc. |
| Sampler (no. 25) | D'Artagnan the French Angelfish | D'Artagnan, Gladiator, the Spanish Hogfish, Sergeant Majors, Wrasses, parrotfish. |
| Forest (no. 16) | Yellowtail Snappers and Black Durgons | Coneys, Graysbys |
| Angel City (no. 6) | Yellowtail Snappers | Yellowtail Snappers, Coneys. |
| Karpata (no. 39) | Yellowtail Snappers | Yellowtail Snappers, Coneys. |
| Cliff (no. 31) | Yellowtail Snappers | Spanish Hogfish (on or near the drop-off) |

One note of caution about fish feeding is very important: we advise you NOT to use fish (fresh or canned) for feeding, at least not before having a serious discussion with your dive guide. Bonaire has numerous moray eels, many of them accustomed to being fed and quite unafraid of people. A diver with fish for food is likely to be found by one . . . or two . . . or more very excited fast moving Spotted Morays. Most of the time the diver would have preferred the eels to be a little less frisky, which they would have been if the food was hot dogs or cheese. We hope this word to the wise is sufficient.

# Common and scientific names

**List of common and scientific names of invertebrates and algae mentioned in the text, with synonyms used by different authors (author's names in parenthesis). Numbers refer to page numbers of relevant illustrations.**

|  |  |
|---|---|
| Arrow Crab (Colin, Kaplan, Voss, Zeiller) | *Stenorhynchus seticornis* |
| Banded Coral Shrimp (Kaplan, Voss, Zeiller) | *Stenopus hispidus*<br>syn: Red-banded Coral Shrimp (Colin), Barber Pole Shrimp (Kaplan) |
| Basket Starfish (Colin, Voss) *85* | *Astrophyton muricatum*<br>syn: Basket Star (Kaplan, Zeiller) |
| Black and White Sea Lily (Kaplan) *24, 96* | *Nemaster grandi* |
| black coral *64, 72, 96, 118, 129* | Collective name for species belonging to the Antipatharia |
| Black Sea Rod (Cairns, Voss) | *Plexaura homomalla*<br>syn: Prostaglandin Plexaura (Voss), Common Bushy Soft Coral (Kaplan) |
| Black Wire Coral (Kaplan) *64, 118* | *Stichopathes lutkeni* |
| Blushing Star Coral (Greenberg) | *Stephanocoenia michelinii* |
| brain coral *18, 123* | Collective name used (in this book) to indicate Smooth-, Knobby-, Grooved-, and Giant Brain Coral |
| Butterprint Brain Coral (Greenberg) *58* | *Meandrina meandrites*<br>syn: Tan Brain Coral (Kaplan), Brain Coral (Zeiller) |
| Cavernous Star Coral (Greenberg) *84* | *Montastrea cavernosa*<br>syn: Large Star Coral (Voss, Zeiller) Large-cupped Boulder Coral (Kaplan) |
| Chocolate-lined Top-shell (Warmke & Abbott) | *Calliostoma javanicum*<br>syn: Chocolate-lined Top Snail (Kaplan) |
| Christmas Tree Worm (Colin) | *Spirobranchus giganteus*<br>syn: Horned Feather Worm (Voss) Horned Christmas Tree Worm, Feathered Christmas Tree Worm (Kaplan) |
| Club Finger Coral (Greenberg) *68* | *Porites porites*<br>syn: Clubbed Finger Coral (Voss, Zeiller) Thick Finger Coral (Kaplan) |

| | |
|---|---|
| Common Lettuce Slug (Voss) *75* | *Tridachia crispata*<br>syn: Lettuce Sea Slug (Kaplan)<br>Ribbon Nudibranch (Zeiller)<br>Ruffleback Nudibranch |
| Common Sea Fan (Cairns, Greenberg, Voss) *40, 120* | *Gorgonia ventalina*<br>*syn: Sea Fan (Colin, Kaplan)* |
| *Coral Crab* (Colin, Kaplan, Voss) | *Carpilius corallinus*<br>syn: Queen Crab (Voss),<br>Bat Crab (Zeiller) |
| Corky Sea Finger (Cairns, Kaplan, Voss) | *Briareum asbestinum*<br>syn: Common Briareum (Cairns, Voss),<br>Dead Man's Fingers (Kaplan) |
| Crustose coralline algae *116* | collective name for several species of algae, belonging, to the genera *Porolithon, Hydrolithon, Lithophyllum* and *Archaeolithothamnion* (see also glossary.) |
| Deepwater Gorgonian (Cairns) *73, 78* | *Iciligorgia schrammi*<br>syn: Schramm's Iciligorgia (Cairns),<br>Deepwater Lace Coral (Kaplan) |
| Dichotomous Black Coral (this book) *72, 96* | *Antipathes dichotoma* |
| Do-not-touch-me Sponge (Voss) *101, 138* | *Neofibularia nolitangere*<br>syn: Touch-me-not Sponge (Kaplan) |
| Dry Sea Plume (Cairns, Voss) | *Pseudopterogorgia acerosa*<br>syn: Sea Feather (Kaplan),<br>Purple Sea Plume (Voss) |
| Elkhorn Coral (Colin, Greenberg, Kaplan, Voss, Zeiller) *19, 27, 90* | *Acropora palmata* |
| Elliptical Star Coral (Greenberg) | *Dichocoenia stokesi*<br>syn: Star Coral (Voss),<br>Stokes' Starlet Coral (Kaplan),<br>Domed Star Coral (Zeiller) |
| Encrusting Colonial Anemone (Kaplan) | *Palythoa caribaeorum* |
| Encrusting Gorgonian (Cairns) *80* | *Erythropodium caribaeorum*<br>syn: Brown Encrusting Soft Coral (Kaplan) |

| | |
|---|---|
| Encrusting Stinging Coral (Greenberg) *138* | *Millepora alcicornis*<br>syn: Stinging Coral, Fire Coral (Voss, Zeiller), Crenelated Fire Coral (Kaplan) |
| false plexaura (Cairns, Kaplan) *54* | Collective name for gorgonian species belonging to the genus *Pseudoplexaura* |
| Fire coral (Colin) *91, 109, 138* | Collective name for Encrusting-, Leafy-, and Square Stinging Coral |
| Fire Worm (Colin) *139* | *Hermodice carunculata*<br>syn: Green Bristle Worm (Voss), Bristle Worm (Greenberg), Fireworm (Kaplan) |
| Flame Helmet (Warmke & Abbott) | *Cassis flammea* |
| Flower Coral (Colin, Greenberg, Kaplan, Voss, Zeiller) *67* | *Eusmilia fastigiata* |
| fungus coral (Greenberg) | Collective name for species belonging to the genus *Mycetophyllia*<br>syn: Cactus Coral (Kaplan) |
| Fused Staghorn Coral (Greenberg) *103* | *Acropora prolifera* |
| Giant Brain Coral (Greenberg) *123* | *Colpophyllia natans*<br>syn: Large Grooved Brain Coral (Kaplan) |
| gorgonians *40, 54, 73, 78, 80, 85* | Collective name for a group of species belonging to the Octocorals<br>syn: soft corals (see also glossary) |
| Grooved Brain Coral (Greenberg) | *Diploria labyrinthiformis*<br>syn: Brain Coral (Voss, Zeiller), Depressed Brain Coral (Kaplan) |
| head corals | Collective name used to indicate a variety of coral species that form 'heads' (star corals, starlet corals, brain corals) |
| Knobby Brain Coral (Greenberg) *18* | *Diploria clivosa*<br>syn: Knobbed Brain Coral (Voss), Sharp-hilled Brain Coral (Kaplan) |

| | |
|---|---|
| Leaf Coral (Greenberg) *65* | *Agaricia agaricites*<br>syn: Lettuce Coral (Voss),<br>Tan Lettuce-leaf Coral (Kaplan) |
| Leafy Stinging Coral (Greenberg) *109* | *Millepora complanata*<br>syn: Flat-topped Fire Coral (Kaplan),<br>Stinging Coral (Zeiller) |
| Little Brown Spotted Shrimp (this book) | *Thor amboinensis* |
| Long-spined Sea Urchin<br>(Colin, Greenberg, Zeiller) *29, 139* | *Diadema antillarum*<br>syn: Long-spined Urchin (Voss),<br>Long-spined Black Urchin (Kaplan) |
| Mountainous Star Coral (Greenberg)<br>*21, 50, 125, 126* | *Montastrea annularis*<br>syn: Star Coral (Colin),<br>Boulder Coral (Kaplan) |
| Music Volute (Warmke & Abbott) | *Voluta musica* |
| Mustard Hill Coral (Greenberg) | *Porites astreoides*<br>syn: Porous Coral (Voss),<br>Yellow Porous Coral (Kaplan),<br>Yellow Porites (Zeiller) |
| Nodding Plexaurella (Cairns) | *Plexaurella nutans*<br>syn: Sea Rod (Kaplan), for all<br>species of Plexaurella |
| Orange Sea Lily (Kaplan) | *Nemaster rubiginosa* |
| Orange Tube Coral (Greenberg)<br>*52, 86, 140* | *Tubastrea coccinea*<br>syn: Red Coral, Orange Coral (Kaplan) |
| Pederson's Cleaning Schrimp<br>(Colin, Kaplan, Voss) | *Periclimenes pedersoni*<br>syn: Ghost Shrimp (Voss),<br>Peterson Shrimp (Zeiller) |
| Pillar Coral (Colin, Greenberg,<br>Kaplan, Voss, Zeiller) *109* | *Dendrogyra cylindrus* |
| Pink-tipped Anemone (Voss) *22, 30* | *Condylactis gigantea*<br>syn: Giant Caribbean Anemone (Kaplan),<br>Sea Anemone (Zeiller) |
| Pinnate Black Coral (this book) *129* | *Antipathes pennacea* |
| Portuguese Man of War (Greenberg,<br>Kaplan, Voss, Zeiller) | *Physalia physalis* |

| | |
|---|---|
| Purple Bleeding Sponge (Voss) *99* | *Iotrochota birotulata*<br>syn: Black Bush Sponge (Kaplan) |
| Purple Tube Sponge (this book) *56, 112* | *Aplysina archeri* |
| Queen Conch (Colin, Kaplan, Warmke & Abbott, Zeiller) | *Strombus gigas* |
| Red Boring Sponge (Kaplan) *29* | *Cliona delitrix* |
| Ringed Anemone (Kaplan, Voss, Zeiller) | *Bartholomea annulata* |
| Rock Boring Urchin (Voss) | *Echinometra lucunter*<br>syn: Red Rock Urchin (Kaplan)<br>Rock Urchin (Zeiller) |
| Rough Lima (Colin, Warmke & Abbott, Zeiller) | *Lima scabra*<br>syn: Rough File Clam (Kaplan) |
| sea fans *40, 73, 78, 120* | Collective name for fan-shaped gorgonians |
| sea plumes *85* | Collective name used for gorgonian species belonging to the genus *Pseudopterogorgia* |
| Sea Rod (Cairns, Voss) | *Plexaura flexuosa*<br>syn: Tan Bushy Soft Coral (Kaplan) |
| sea wasps (Colin, Kaplan) | Collective name for species of jellyfish belonging to the genus *Carybdea* |
| Scroll Coral (Greenberg) | *Agaricia undata* |
| Sheet Coral (Greenberg) *67, 94, 95* | *Agaricia lamarcki* and *Agaricia grahamae* (distinction in the field between these two species is difficult). Syn: Lamarck's Lettuce Leaf Coral (Kaplan) |
| Short Coral-shell (Warmke & Abbott) | *Coralliophila abbreviata*<br>syn: Short Coral Snail (Kaplan) |
| Shovel-nosed Lobster (Voss) | *Scyllarides aequinoctialis*<br>syn: Spanish Lobster (Voss, Colin) |
| Slimy Sea Plume (Cairns, Voss) | *Pseudopterogorgia americana*<br>syn: Sea Feather (Kaplan) |
| Slipper Lobster (Kaplan, Voss) | *Scyllarides nodifer*<br>syn: Ridged Slipper Lobster (Colin, Voss) |

| | |
|---|---|
| Smooth Brain Coral (Greenberg) | *Diploria strigosa*<br>syn: Common Brain Coral<br>Kaplan, Zeiller) |
| Smooth Starlet Coral<br>(Greenberg) | *Siderastrea siderea*<br>syn: Shallow-water Starlet Coral (Kaplan) |
| Spiny Lobster (Colin, Greenberg, Kaplan<br>Voss, Zeiller *110* | *Panulirus argus*<br>syn: Crawfish (Voss) |
| Spotted Cleaning Shrimp<br>(Kaplan, Voss, Zeiller) | *Periclimenes yucatanicus* |
| Square Stinging Coral (Greenberg) | *Millepora squarrosa*<br>syn: Encrusting Fire Coral (Kaplan) |
| Staghorn Coral (Colin, Greenberg,<br>Kaplan, Voss, Zeiller) *19, 30* | *Acropora cervicornis* |
| Sun Anemone (Kaplan, Zeiller) *119* | *Stoichactis helianthus* |
| symbiotic colonial anemones (Kaplan) | Collective name for a number of species<br>belonging to the genus *Parazoanthus*<br>(primarily growing on sponges) |
| Tub Sponge (Kaplan) *41* | *Xestospongia muta*<br>syn: Basket Sponge (Kaplan)<br>Barrel Sponge (Colin) |
| worm shells (Warmke & Abbott) | Collective name for species belonging to<br>the group of the Vermetidae, coiled,<br>worm-like snails |
| Yellow Boring Sponge (Kaplan) | *Siphonodictyon coralliphagum* |
| Yellow Pencil Coral (Greenberg) *20* | *Madracis mirabilis*<br>syn: Branching Coral (Kaplan) |

# Glossary

*Beachrock* - material of different sizes deposited on beaches and lithified.

*Bioerosion* - process whereby individual coral colonies, or the reef framework as a whole, is affected (eroded) by biological activities such as boring and grazing, sometimes in combination with biochemical solution.

*Buttresses* - coral promontories with high coral cover running down from the drop-off along the reef slope, growing seaward and alternated by valleys with low coral cover through which sediment is transported down the reef slope.

*Calcareous* - containing calcium carbonate (limestone).

*Coelenterates* (present name: Cnidarians) - group of rather primitive animals to which jellyfish, anemones, gorgonians, corals and black corals belong. Two basic types are distinguished: the attached polyp with tentacles and mouth facing upward and the unattached medusa (jellyfish) with a bell-shaped body and tentacles and mouth facing downward. Nearly all Coelenterates have nematocysts (stinging apparatus) in their tentacles.

*Crinoids* (sea lilies) - group of animals belonging to the Echinoderms. Reef-dwelling crinoids are mobile and have a series of arms that can be extended to strain food particles from the water (filter-feeding).

*Crustaceans* - group of animals to which shrimps, lobster and crabs belong. Crustaceans usually have a pair of claws and their bodies are protected by a cover of chitin.

*Crustose coralline algae* (encrusting coralline algae, calcareous algae) - red algae that build limestone structures. Important as reef builders because they consolidate loose limestone fragments and cover fixed substrates, making them impenatrable to boring organisms. In areas with high wave action they can create algal ridges that reach up to the surface.

*Drop-off* - increase in angle of the reef face over a relatively short distance (e.g. transitional area between shallow reef terrace and reef slope).

*Echinoderms* - group of animals to which sea stars, sea urchins, sea cucumbers and sea lilies belong. Characteristic for the Echinoderms is a water-vascular system, a hydraulic system which is used to extend or contract a large number of tube feet. The tube feet serve for attachment and locomotion. The structure of Echinoderms shows a radial symmetry of five (or multiples of five) parts (arms, skeleton plates, etc.)

*Ecosystem* - system of living and non-living components acting together in a functional manner.

*Genus* - one but lowest subdivision in the nomenclature to characterize a group of organisms that have certain features in common. A genus includes several *species* (at least one).

*Gorgonians* (soft corals) - group of animals belonging to the Octocorals, a subgroup of the Coelenterates. The polyps of Octocorals bear eight tentacles and their tissues contain small skeletal elements (spicules) of calcium carbonate. In addition the majority of gorgonians has a central supporting cylinder, composed of horny or calcareous material.

*Isopods* - elongated, flattened crustaceans, many of which are parasitic.

*Lower reef slope* - lower part of the steep slope of the fringing reef from about 24-27 m (80-90 ft) down.

*Mesenterial filament* - cord-like extension of the vertical partitions in the body of a polyp; contains nematocysts and has a digestive function.

*Mollusks* - large group of animals to which seashells, snails, sea slugs, octopus and squid belong. Most Mollusks possess a shell, however in some groups the shell is absent or reduced (slugs, octopus and squid). Most Mollusks have a muscular foot, a mantle, that forms the shell. Some Mollusks have a rasp-like 'tongue' with which algae can be scraped off the rocks.

*Nematocysts* - stinging apparatus in the tentacles of Coelenterates, consisting of a 'spear' that is fired upon contact with any foreign object and injects a venom into a prey organism.

*Oscules* - pore-like openings in sponges through which the water flow leaves the sponge.

*Photosynthesis* - biochemical process whereby carbon dioxide and water combine to form carbohydrates and oxygen in the presence of light and chlorophyll.

*Pinnate* - feather-like.

*Reef-building corals* - (hermatypic corals) - corals that possess zooxanthellae and are capable of depositing limestone in sufficient quantities to form reefs.

*Reef slide* - phenomenon occurring on steep reefs, whereby part of the reef face breaks loose at the drop-off and slides down the reef slope; factors that influence the occurrence of reef slides are the weight of the living coral strata, the slope angle, the degree of consolidation of underlying strata and the degree to which coral colonies are affected by boring organisms.

*Sawah-bench* - surf bench formed by crustose coralline algae and worm shells in the sea-air interface on steep limestone cliffs of the windward coast; the bench represents an area of retarded erosion.

*Shallow terrace* - gently sloping submarine terrace of the fringing reef, from the shore down to the drop-off.

*Soft corals* - see gorgonians.

*Species* - lowest subdivision in the nomenclature of the animal and plant kingdom; each species name consists of two names: the first is the genus name, the second is characteristic for a particular plant or animal that belongs to this genus. The combination of the two names is unique to one particular organism. Example: *Montastrea annularis* (Mountainous Star Coral) and *Montastrea cavernosa* (Cavernous Star Coral) are two distinct species belonging to the genus *Montastrea*.

*Spurs* - ridges on the shallow terrace in areas of strong water movement, oriented perpendicular to the wave front and formed by seaward and upward growth of corals and/ or by erosive forces; spurs are closely spaced together and separated by sandy grooves in which no coral growth occurs.

*Stony corals* (Scleractinians) - group of Coelenterates, many of which colonial, that build a limestone skeleton.

*Symbiosis* - a relationship of favorable or unfavorable nature between different species.

*Upper reef slope* - upper part of the steep slope of the fringing reef, from the drop-off down to about 24-27 m (80-90 ft).

*White band disease* - coral disease occurring among Staghorn and Elkhorn coral, possibly related to bacteria in the coral tissue, manifesting itself as white bands (the freshly killed coral tissue) along the branches.

*Zooxanthellae* - unicellular algae living in symbiosis with coral polyps.

## Suggestions for further reading


Boer, B.A. de, D. Hoogerwerf, I. Kristensen and J.C. Post. 1973. Antillean Fish Guide, Netherlands Antilles National Parks Foundation, Curaçao, Netherlands Antilles.

Cairns, S. and G.L. Voss. 1977. A Guide to the Commoner Shallow-water Gorgonians of Florida, the Gulf of Mexico and the Caribbean Region. Sea Grant Field Guide Series no. 6. University of Miami Sea Grant Program, Miami, Fla.

Chaplin, Charles C.G., and P. Scott. 1973. Fishwatchers Guide. Livingston Publishing Company, Wynnewood, Pa.

Colin, P.L., 1979. Caribbean Reef Invertebrates and Plants. T.F.H. Publications, Jersey City, N.J.

Goodson, G. 1976. The Many Splendored Fishes of the Atlantic Coast Including the Fish of the Gulf of Mexico, Florida, Bermuda, The Bahamas and the Caribbean. Marquest Colorguide Books, Palos Verdes Estates, Calif.

Greenberg, I., 1977. Guide to Corals and Fishes. Seahawk Press, Miami, Fla.

Kaplan, Eugene H., 1982. A Field Guide to Coral Reefs. Houghton Mifflin Company, Boston.

Nagelkerken, W., 1980. Coral Reef Fishes. Island Territory of Curaçao, Netherlands Antilles.

Opresko, L., D. Opresko, R. Thomas and G.L. Voss. 1973. Guide to the Lobsters and Lobster-like animals of Florida, the Gulf of Mexico and the Caribbean Region. Sea Grant Field Guide Series no. 1. University of Miami Sea Grant Program, Miami, Fla.

Opresko, L., R. Thomas, F.M. Bayer and G.L. Voss. 1976. A Guide to the Larger Marine Gastropods of Florida, the Gulf of Mexico and the Caribbean Region Sea Grant Field Guide Series no. 5. University of Miami Sea Grant Program, Miami, Fla.

Randall, John E., 1968. Caribbean Reef Fishes. T.F.H. Publications, Jersey City, N.J.

Smith, F.G. Walton, 1971. Atlantic Reef Corals. University of Miami Press, Coral Gables, Fla.

Stokes, F.J. 1980. Handguide to the Coral Reef Fishes of the Caribbean and Adjacent Tropical Waters Including Florida, Bermuda and the Bahamas. Lippincott and Crowell, Publishers, New York.

Voss, Gilbert L., 1976. Seashore Life of Florida and the Caribbean. E.A. Seemann Publishing Inc., Miami, Fla.

Voss, G.L., L. Opresko and R. Thomas. 1973. The Potentially Commercial Species of Octopus and Squid in Florida, the Gulf of Mexico and the Caribbean Area. Sea Grant Field Guide Series no 2. University of Miami Sea Grant Program, Miami, Fla.

Warmke, Germaine L. and R.T. Abbott. 1975. Caribbean Seashells. Dover Publications Inc., New York.

Zeiller, W., 1974. Tropical Marine Invertebrates of Southern Florida and the Bahama Islands. John Wiley, New York.